D0374917

SEARCHING for A MUSTARD SEED

MIRIAM SAGAN

SEARCHING *for* A MUSTARD SEED

One Young Widow's Unconventional Story

QUALITY WORDS IN PRINT

Searching for a Mustard Seed
One Young Widow's Unconventional Story

by Miriam Sagan

Copyright © 2003 Miriam Sagan
Published by Quality Words In Print, LLC
P. O. Box 2704, Costa Mesa, California 92628-2704
www.qwipbooks.com

Interior Design & Typesetting by Desktop Miracles, Inc., Stowe, VT

LCCN: 2002095379

First Edition

Publisher's Cataloging-in-Publication
(Provided by Quality Books, Inc.)

Sagan, Miriam, 1954–
     Searching for a mustard seed: one young widow's unconventional story / by Miriam Sagan.
          p.   cm.
     ISBN 0–9713160–3–1

1. Sagan, Miriam, 1954–   2. Poets, American—20th century—Biography.
3. Buddhism.   4. Bereavement.   5. Grief.   6. Widows—New Mexico—Santa Fe—Biography.   7. Santa Fe (N. M.)—Biography.   I. Title.

PS3569.A288Z477   2003   811'.54
                                                                          QBI33-903

Printed in the United States of America

Certain sections of this book appeared, in a different form, in the following publications: Are We There Yet, Bogg Magazine, The Christian Science Monitor, Hip Mama, Sage Magazine/Albuquerque Journal.

Thanks to Ahsahta Press, Red Hen, and Lilliput/Modest Proposal Chapbooks where the poems first appeared.

All gratitude and love to my friends who allowed themselves to be portrayed here. And most of all—to Richard Feldman.

Contents

The Sick Man: an Introduction

Looking back, I think that my first husband, Robert Winson, was ill the entire time I knew him. We met in San Francisco; he was twenty-two years old, I was twenty-seven. He was a skinny, Jewish guy from New Jersey, just my type, smart and funny, with a long, unkempt beard and thick glasses framing his big, brown, myopic eyes. We shared friends and interests; we could hang around endlessly together.

We were married in 1982, and two years later moved to Santa Fe, New Mexico, where we settled and bought a house.

In late 1988, when I was hugely pregnant with our daughter Isabel, Robert began to experience severe abdominal pain and bleeding. Sometimes he would simply stand up and leave a frightening trail of blood on the floor. He was soon diagnosed with a moderate case of ulcerative colitis, an unpleasant, but not apparently life-threatening, disease, one in which the colon had an auto-immune reaction and devoured itself.

"You know, I think I've been sick for years with something like this," he said soon after the diagnosis.

I also remembered his bouts of illness, vomiting and diarrhea, pain. Nine months pregnant, I was focused on preparing for the birth of my child. But some small, terrifying voice spoke up inside me, saying sharply, "Someday you'll look back on this and think, 'This is when it began'."

Of course, I ignored the voice. I needed Robert more than I ever had before. But the voice had been right.

Robert recovered from his first bout and was able to coach me in childbirth.

Colitis, by its nature, is a disease of episodes and remissions. Although he had flare-ups, the situation remained fairly benign. Still, reading his journals after his death, I was struck by how many times he recorded the ominous "shitting blood,"—often after a stressful event. He was functional, but not completely well.

In 1993, when our daughter was four and Robert was thirty-four, he took a decided turn for the worse. For months he was apparently quite ill, but refused to go to the doctor. By the autumn of that year, he was close to being incapacitated. In early 1994, my frantic nagging and the fact that he obviously wasn't getting better propelled him to see his own doctor and a specialist.

This was the start of more intensive medical treatment. He was put on prednisone, that volatile cortisone drug, which certainly stops inflammation, but which made him moon-faced and bloated, sensitive to light and noise, not himself. Robert also tried any experimental drug for colitis he had heard of—a nicotine patch, which some studies showed had helped—and eventually injections of the chemotherapy drug, Methatrexate, which had shown some success in treating auto-immune diseases such as psoriasis and colitis. His cluster of prescription bottles soon numbered well over a dozen, from vitamins to anti-diarrhea drugs and eventually to the appetite-increasing drug Marinol.

Robert did not get better. He grew weaker. He was in bed much of the day, housebound for days, even weeks, at a time. Ordinary life and activities were too much of an effort and soon an impossibility. The photographs of him at our daughter's fifth birthday party show an emaciated man with greenish skin tone. By that summer, he had lost his job. An entire year dragged by with him neither recovering nor getting obviously worse. We were in a terrifying limbo.

In the summer of 1995, it became obvious to those around him that Robert was beginning to seriously deteriorate. In an extremely unusual move for a doctor, his general practitioner called and told him, "Robert, I am very worried about you. I dreamed about you, and that is not a good sign."

She and his specialist began to recommend the option of surgery, which would cure the colitis once and for all. Many strides had been made since Robert's grandfather had had such surgery for colon cancer, a disease with a genetic component, and had frightened Robert as a child. It was actually two surgeries: The first would remove his colon, and a few months later, reconstructive surgery would eliminate his need to wear a bag. He would be healed.

Of course, that was not the case. Robert collapsed several days before his scheduled surgery. He had been given a shunt in his chest and was on intravenous feedings at home with the help of a visiting nurse. But this was not enough. He landed in the local hospital and was eventually transported to Presbyterian Hospital in Albuquerque for the scheduled surgery.

The night he collapsed, I spoke to his GP on the phone. "Do you thing he's dying?" I asked.

"No, Miriam. All of his tests look normal. He's just very weak."

"You'll tell me if you think he is terminal?"

"Of course, of course."

Later, she would write me a beautiful condolence letter, saying, "Some patients a doctor will always find haunting, and Robert was one of them." She continued to write me notes for several years, proving herself an unusually compassionate person, not to mention physician.

Robert had surgery on October 10, 1995. It was our wedding anniversary, which went uncelebrated.

Coming back into consciousness, he said two odd things. First, quoting the Grateful Dead song, he said, "What a long strange trip it's been." Then, making a joke, he imitated the Tin Man in the movie of "The Wizard of Oz," squeaking out "oil can" because his lips seemed frozen.

Still, he was soon walking around, visiting with friends, and fascinated by a science program he'd seen on new theories about the dinosaurs.

Ten days later, his heart stopped, and he went into a coma. That is where this story begins.

When I was eighteen years old and a freshman at Harvard University, I had an unsettling experience in the stacks of Lamont Library. At that time I was close to emotional hysteria caused by the fact that I was conducting two love affairs simultaneously. I didn't know what to do or who to choose. I was overwhelmed, while holding down an advanced course of study. Surely, I thought, there must be some book to help me. I started looking, but in 1973, there weren't many books about young women in my situation, although soon there would be hundreds. On the cusp of feminist publishing, I could find nothing but some overly sad Doris Lessing books. I started to cry. I had spent my whole life reading, and now it seemed there was nothing helpful to read.

The situation repeated itself after Robert died. I was now a widow. Although a grief counselor told me she abhorred the label, I did not mind it myself. I liked that it meant "empty," which was how I felt. I liked that the feminine was the standard form, as men tended to die before their wives. I even liked that there was a sexy undergarment called a "merry widow." But I needed more than a label; I needed a story—a narrative—of what had happened to me.

Stories themselves can be said to be therapeutic, but like the mere passage of time, narrative is not enough. In my grief group, I listened to some people tell an unchanging, compulsive story of what had happened to them, over and over. This was not the story I wanted to tell myself. After Robert died, I would tell myself, *This is not the last thing that is going to happen to you.* I wanted neither my life nor my story frozen in amber.

The books I took out of the library with the word "widow" in the title did not seem to apply to me. My life was too different from the middle-class, middle-aged or elderly women whose concerns were addressed there. I did not care deeply about life insurance or how to go to dinner parties alone. I cared about dating, weightlifting, and my startling shifts of consciousness.

Born in 1954, I considered myself a quintessential baby boomer. I was in the middle of a demographic bulge. When I was a teenager, everyone was a teenager; when I had a baby, everyone had babies. Now I was a widow, and no one else seemed to be. We were a generation that knew little about death.

"Thank God for Dr. Salk," was the mantra my mother repeated every summer. She had lived through polio epidemics and had seen cousins and friends crippled. My mother, who was born before antibiotics and vaccines, praised the century and developed nation that pretty much guaranteed infants would live and mothers survive childbirth. Of course, my grandparents had died, but they were old, and I had been a child.

The AIDS epidemic had knocked my generation off its secure belief that we would lead long and healthy lives. And, as I learned after I was widowed, more of my friends and acquaintances had experienced the loss of someone close than I had ever paid attention to.

Still, when it came to the death of a young man, we were novices. Perhaps, we secretly believed that if we got enough exercise and ate enough tofu, death would give us a generational dispensation, and we would live forever.

The people around me may not have had a deep acquaintance with death, but they regarded it in true boomer fashion—as an extreme state to be experienced. Robert's death, cremation, and memorial services all had a wild, party aspect to them, as well as one of intense grief. The people who loved him were an unconventional lot—Zen priests, painters, poets, composers, rock-and-rollers—but he also knew librarians, attorneys, and housewives.

Our friend Kathleen, sitting in my house before the funeral, sobbed, "This is like a wedding . . . only *much much* worse."

Indeed, there was a curious quality of entering a ritual, almost celebratory time, of being unstuck from daily life and its patterns and concerns.

The circle of people around me also included more traditional and old-fashioned people. My friends and family members over sixty certainly knew more about death than I did. My neighbors, traditional Hispanic New Mexicans, treated me with a particular kindness and decorum that grew out of a more-than-passing acquaintance with suffering. When I decided to remarry, these were the most supportive people. My contemporaries were shocked; they expected more fidelity to the dead, in part because they had less understanding of the irrevocable nature of such loss.

It was my elderly friend Elizabeth, born in Kansas, who said simply of my engagement, "Well, dear, you need an interest in life."

I wrote this book to tell my story. I wrote it because my contemporaries will not live forever and because grief is either a path we have trod or will have trod. I wrote it so that some woman like me might find a friendlier book on the shelf.

And I also wrote it to talk to Robert, my dead husband. For although the dead don't speak too frequently to us, we continue to speak to them. I still see him often in my dreams. Sometimes he feels like an obvious projection of my unconscious mind; at times, he feels like a visitation from a spirit world in which I neither believe nor disbelieve. Just the other night, he informed me he was attending nursing school as a new career, and I was delighted to see his stack of textbooks.

"I'm sure you'll make a good nurse," I said, "after all you've been through."

"But I need you to move to San Francisco to support me financially," he said, awakening an argument we had had too many times in life.

Robert has been dead for seven years, a time beyond any prescribed cycle of grief. Still, I can't help but look for clues to whether or not he knew how ill he was. Throughout the course of his illness, he rarely spoke about it and discouraged me from bringing up the topic.

After his death, I browsed through his notebooks, both hoping for and fearing disclosure. His journals weren't diaries, but rather jottings of things that interested him or caught his fancy. Towards the end of his last notebook, his handwriting was visibly deteriorated. Robert was proud of his clear, bold handwriting and had, at times, practiced calligraphy. But the drugs he took, particularly the prednisone, as well as the disease itself, had made his hands unsure and shaky.

There, on the last page of the notebook, copied out in an uneven hand, was one of Shakespeare's sonnets in its entirety. I looked it up; it was Sonnet 140, which began:

"Be wise as thou art cruel; do not press
My tongue-tied patience with too much disdain;
Lest sorrow lend me words, and words express
The manner of my pity-wanting pain."

It was not an auspicious start. The sonnet might be about a scornful lover, but it also seemed to embody pain, physical pain. When I came to lines seven and eight, I felt the shock of understanding:

"As testy sick men, when their deaths be near,
No news but health from their physicians know . . ."

I started sobbing when I read this couplet. So, I realized, Robert had known he was dying, known more than his doctors, who had maintained a careful optimism; it was there in black and white, in William Shakespeare's words.

And then came the saddest part:

"For, if I should despair, I should grow mad,
And in my madness might speak ill of thee."

Robert had indeed spoken ill of me when he was sick. At times, his criticisms had seemed endless, unbearable. Our daughter Isabel and I were so noisy, I didn't wash the dishes properly, I bought the wrong soup. Was I trying to kill him? He had once actually asked that in a fit of exasperation.

His dependence on me—physical, emotional, financial— was unspoken and unexamined. Yet it enraged him. On the way to the doctor's office for an unpleasant test, which required anesthesia, he hit me on the arm—hard—when I couldn't find a convenient parking space.

If I had fleeting thoughts of leaving him, they were immediately quelled by my sense of loyalty and by my genuine love for him. Besides, I realized full well, without me, he would be homeless, destitute. To view our relationship with any questions at all was terrifying. I was committed to caring for him, even when neither of us admitted that was what I was doing.

The sonnet ended on the usual upbeat note of Shakespeare's trying to tie it all together. But the impression it left with me, in the context of Robert's notebook, was much more the line:

"Now this ill-wresting world is grown so bad . . ."

The world had indeed grown bad for him, a narrow painful place, one he often endured stoically, even cheerfully, until the rage burst through. Still, at the end, the sonnet exhorted:

"Bear thine eyes straight."

And that is the real reason I wrote this book, not so much to understand Robert, but to understand myself, to make a story, and to make sense of all the things that subsequently happened to me.

Coma

"You were planning to eat
Three bowls of rice
In the land of the dead.
Sweetheart, your expression
Didn't inspire me with confidence—
You seemed too pleased
To go."

"ORIOKI" FROM *The Widow's Coat*

"Mrs. Winson," said the voice on the phone, "your husband's heart has stopped."

For a moment, I did not realize the voice was talking to me. It was the first—and last—time over the course of a thirteen-year marriage that I would be called by my husband's name. Then it sunk in. It was Robert whose heart had stopped. My husband, who ten days before had been admitted to Albuquerque's Presbyterian

Hospital for colon surgery. Robert, whom I had seen the day before. Robert, who had left me a late-night phone message on the machine: *I love you.* Robert's heart had stopped.

I started shaking, and I must have started screaming, because our six-year-old daughter Isabel appeared from her room, saying, "Mommy. Mommy."

"It's nothing," I said brusquely. "Get dressed for school."

The surgeon was on the phone, speaking clearly over the sixty miles between Albuquerque and Santa Fe. "During rounds this morning, I noticed Robert's lips were blue. I asked him if it was O.K. to move him to Intensive Care, and he said 'O.K.' As we were moving him, he went into cardiac arrest. I've resuscitated him, but he is in a coma. I'm taking him into surgery. I suggest you come immediately."

I literally could not speak. I was stammering into the phone, "Uh, uh, I, I . . ."

He had said "O.K.," I thought. How like Robert. O.K., O.K., be cool, everything is fine. His last word: O.K. It was then I knew he would die. But really, I had known for a long time.

"Don't drive yourself," the surgeon told me. "DON'T DRIVE YOURSELF. Get a friend to drive," he was shouting.

"I'm going to call our families," I said.

"Don't call your families. Just come."

"I'm going to call the families," I said again. "On the East Coast. So they can get here." I hated the surgeon. As I hung up, I didn't even feel the urge to be polite to him on the off chance that he could save Robert's life.

Robert was already gone.

I would not drive myself. I called my friend Hope. She was tall and competent, she had children and a good four-wheel-drive vehicle, and she could shoot a gun and produce a movie. I always thought that if I had to fight the Nazis or some analogous terror, I would want to be with Hope. Her name said it all.

Hope appeared, drove Isabel to school, and together we started the long drive south to Albuquerque. I felt completely stoned and disoriented as we sped through a familiar and spectacular landscape of mesas and mountains, vast far views, and wind-blown rock formations. We cruised down from the high plateau where the city of Santa Fe sat, down the steep La Bajada Hill where wagon-train passengers had had to get out to walk, past the Indian Pueblos of Cochiti and Santo Domingo, and into the congested traffic of Albuquerque.

It was October, and the blue sky was hazy with traffic smog and heat. Hope was on the cell phone much of the time to her brother, a doctor in practice with Robert's general practitioner. The phone would cut out from time to time in New Mexico fashion, the signal obscured by valleys or foothills. It was the first of a series of interrupted conversations.

Soon, a little group of Robert's friends were assembled in the antiseptic atmosphere of Presbyterian Hospital. Friends had called each other, rushed to the scene. A half dozen of us huddled together in the waiting room outside surgery. I lay on the thin artificial carpet in a fetal position. Most of Robert's friends were Buddhist practitioners—Zen students like he—both priests and lay people. They maintained a quality of calm, of preparedness in an emergency, sitting quietly.

Among them was my friend Miriam Bobkoff. Since we'd shared a name, it seemed inevitable that we'd become friends. She was also a Zen priest, and she felt an obligation to Robert, who was her Dharma brother.

More familiar to me than Zen calm was my friend Sharon, who had dashed in from her house on the other side of Albuquerque. Curly haired and warm, like me she was a Jewish girl from New Jersey. Throughout the next twelve hours, she would attempt to get me to eat—a bite of a sandwich, a spoonful of yogurt—which was a thankless task.

Robert did not die on the operating table, although by now he was probably already brain dead. He was moved by elevator to the ICU and our group to its waiting room. A mere ten days before, Robert had had his first surgery.

My father had come from the East Coast to help us. There had always been a deep bond between my father and my husband, despite their differences. Robert was a Zen Buddhist priest with a shaved head; my father was an atheist who disliked religion. My father was so anti-religious that he refused even to enter the building that housed San Francisco's Zen Center when we lived in that neighborhood. Although we tried to entice him with the fact that it had been designed by the classic Californian architect, Julia Morgan, he refused to go through the doors of what was to him a house of worship. But my father and husband were both intellectual and bookish; Robert had even taken my father's sociology classes at the University of California.

When my father arrived, Robert was already in a weakened condition. He had collapsed before the scheduled surgery and been hospitalized, then transported by ambulance from Santa Fe to the more major medical center in Albuquerque.

My father and I had shared an anxious vigil on the first surgery, where Robert's colon was removed. My father had kept me going with ice cream, coffee, and his scrappy attitude. That was another thing he and Robert shared: Beneath the intellect, they were both short, tough guys from New Jersey.

To our relief, Robert had recovered from surgery, could walk, joke, and eat a little.

Throughout this, my father had been unusually attuned to the suffering of other patients around us. He felt that an anonymous doctor did not treat Robert's aged roommate with respect, and he was particularly upset by a group of Navajos, who sat for several days outside the ICU. A group of family and friends, they never left their communal posts, and the looks of grief on their faces and occasional uncontrolled sobbing were pitiable.

"Those poor people," my father would say. "Someone young must be dying, maybe in a terrible car crash." He'd speculate and shake his head. Now the Navajos were gone, and my friends and I were in their place, also people who had come from a distance, our faces distorted by grief.

The surgeon and anesthesiologist came out of the ICU to give me the report.

We all got up to face them.

"I need to speak to just the immediate family members," one of the doctors said.

Hope responded, "Anything you have to say, you say to everybody." She asked clear pointed questions, got clear answers.

Robert's odds were plummeting; there were hundreds of blood clots throughout his body. His blood clotting mechanism had gone berserk, a little understood but well-documented condition in post-surgical patients. His internal organs were dying, full of gangrene. He had been transfused to no effect. He was breathing on a respirator. Only his heart was still beating.

We trooped into the ICU to see him.

Later Hope and Sharon remembered how I had ordered them "Come in."

There seemed to be a lot of blood, a nurse even emptied a bucket into the toilet, and then didn't flush it so as not to disturb us, but the blood was disturbing, and Hope remembered she was so frightened of it, she wanted to bolt. But I did not notice the discomfort of my friend.

Robert lay blue in a coma, his freezing body wrapped in warm plastic, his breath kept alive by a machine. That was the first time I saw him as a corpse, a focal point, as the noisy living swirled around him. His tongue lolled out of his mouth, making him hideous. He did not stir.

People dashed in and out, making phone calls.

We needed a senior Zen priest. We needed a professional, someone who wasn't personally involved. Robert himself had been ordained in the Soto lineage by his teacher, Richard Baker-roshi. This line of Zen had been brought to the United States by Senryu Suzuki-roshi, whom Robert had revered but had never met. After that, he had kept his head and face neatly shaved. Now, there was several days' worth of scraggly growth covering his thin face.

I had met Robert in San Francisco when I was twenty-seven and he was twenty-two. This was in the early 80's, when the city was in the last flush of a party that began with the Summer of Love and ended devastatingly with AIDS. Robert had a crush on my blonde roommate and hung around trying to win her affection, which was never forthcoming in the romantic sense. The first time I saw him he was making a sculpture by screwing a wine corkscrew into a large lemon. We fell in love immediately.

It was raining hard in the city the night Robert asked me to marry him, a tropical storm in off the Pacific, blowing hard enough to uproot palm trees. We sat in the Achilles Heel, a bar that is no longer on Haight Street, and I remember I was drinking vodka. Vodka is what I drank the whole time I lived in San Francisco. I ate Russian caviar for free at happy hours and meat piroge wrapped in paper from the deli and drank vodka when I needed something cold you could look right through.

Robert sat across the table from me, skinny, bearded, myopic, charming, and said, "We should get married."

I burst into tears. "You're just saying that to bother me," I sobbed. "We haven't even been to bed together."

He'd refused me, declaring we didn't know each other well enough. I assumed he had some kind of disease. We had only been involved for a few weeks, but in my circles such restraint was unheard of. "Why do you want to marry me?" I asked.

"You are the first woman I ever knew what I wanted her for," he said. "Let's get married. If I'm ever in a coma, I want you to pull the plug."

Gulping vodka in a rainstorm, I said, "Yes."

The waiter came over and kissed Robert on the mouth to congratulate him. That was before we even heard of a gay cancer that turned out to be AIDS and killed our friends and neighbors, when gay waiters kissed straight men, when people who barely knew each other got engaged.

Ten months later, I married Robert. We were married in a formal ceremony in the living room of the Victorian guesthouse at the San Francisco Zen Center. We lit candles together, drank water from a double-mouthed jug, took Buddhist precepts, and exchanged strings of prayer beads instead of rings. I complained that the ceremony was essentially the same as the one used for ordination—I had promised not to kill, instead of love or honor. The priest who married us sprinkled us with the dew of a green leaf. I did not change my last name.

Robert never wanted to be anything except a Zen priest. As a child, he'd read about Jain holy men, who swept the dirt in front of them to avoid killing even tiny insects and thought, *That's the job for me!*

When we first lived together—on Rose Alley in the inner Fillmore—he worked at the Zen Center's grocery store. French bread, raspberry soda, figs, blue cheese, chocolate truffles. We ate well because he had the key, and we kept a handwritten account of what we owed by the cash register.

We were young and poor and did not have a car, and so to get to *Shakespeare in the Park*, we had to hitch a ride from the Bart station to the green amphitheater in the eucalyptus trees. We sat there holding hands and munching as actors turned and declared. That was the first and only time I saw *Antony and Cleopatra*.

Midway through, Robert squeezed my hand and said, "Don't ever die."

At the end I watched in wonder as Cleo hauled Antony on some kind of stage sledge up an obelisk, in which she was preparing to commit suicide. It was late when we got home and dashed that dangerous half block down Rose Alley to our flat where the punk rock band lived beneath us, where drag queens lived across the street, and where someone we didn't want to know left neatly one used condom and one hypodermic needle by the curb early each morning.

Now Robert was dying. I paced the corridor of the ICU.

Sharon had rushed out to get us a rabbi, her friend Lynn Gottlieb. Sharon and I both cared about Judaism, although, of course, Robert had not. He'd always said, "Buddhism is my religion; my tribal affiliation is Judaism." So I knew he wouldn't mind if I needed a rabbi. Sharon had been unable to reach Lynn by phone and finally left a note on Lynn's door, telling her where we were.

Lynn appeared, a famous feminist rabbi with long brown hair and a reassuring manner. I knew Robert would have been pleased at such an unorthodox choice. Lynn sang over his prone body in a beautiful voice, telling his soul to fly free in a mixture of Hebrew and English.

"Don't let this go for too long," she warned me, this state between life and death, implying that it was dangerous for all of us for Robert's soul to be trapped in a limbo state.

"When can I date?" I sobbed my most inappropriate question at her. I couldn't believe this was my question when my husband was dying, but it flew out of my mouth.

"Whenever you want," Rabbi Lynn said. Then she cautioned me that she did not know how to speak to the dead, although sometimes people expected her to because she was a rabbi. She added a last piece of advice, "After he dies, don't leave the body alone until he is buried."

I had felt weirdly single for months. Robert had been seriously ill for two years, often bedridden, and I was used to going out alone, taking care of our daughter alone. Robert and I had not slept in the same bed for a year and a half. I took care of my car; I took care of the accounts.

Still, for much of the time I felt firmly married. We spent hours talking, still made love as frequently as Robert had energy, listened to music, gossiped, consulted about our daughter. In many ways, we felt more connected than many couples I knew who had a routinized practical relationship.

But something had changed a few months before. I found myself flirting with a father on my daughter's school camping trip, complimenting him on his volunteer fireman's jacket. I was even chagrined that he didn't flirt back. I noticed men. I thought twice about finally throwing out a letter from an old boyfriend, a letter that was so long overdue to return I had given up.

"If something happens to Robert, I might need to talk to an old boyfriend like Richard," a voice inside me said. It seemed bizarre, but I left the unanswered letter face up on the top of my desk.

"I have to pull the plug," I kept saying to the consternation of the doctors. The surgeon admitted my husband was probably brain dead but kept insisting, in an unscientific fashion, that he had seen miracles happen. No one understood that I had made a promise a long time ago in the Achilles Heel Bar, a place that no longer existed, in front of a gay waiter, who was probably dead himself. I couldn't stay long in the room.

Rabbi Lynn left, and I continued to make arrangements.

Hope and I conferred. We'd agreed that if Robert didn't die by midafternoon, the time she'd need to go pick up Isabel and her kids from school, she would leave and go without me. I embraced her before she went to drive back up La Bajada Hill to pick up Isabel, keep a calm face, and have Isabel sleep over at her house. It was the first time my six-year-old had slept under a roof without at least one of her parents.

On a return trip through the corridor, I saw the handsome back of a clean-shaven Buddhist priest in robes. The Zen crowd had managed to raise their own clergy. From the back, he looked like Robert.

I slapped my hands together, hard, twice. I decided that if I startled him, he could not enter the room, because he had not shown true awareness. The priest did not flinch. He had passed my test, and I let him into the room. In some startling way, I was acting spontaneously, like someone in a Zen teaching story or koan, rather than like myself.

Jitsudo-sensei turned out to have been a local boy, Spanish, from up north, on Embudo by the river. But his eyebrows were incredibly bushy like a Japanese ink painting of a Zen master. Robert would have liked him. I liked him myself. I wondered if he was single and if he would like to marry me.

It continued to occur to me that not only was Robert dying, but he was *leaving me.* I was going to be alone, single, a widow, with my small daughter.

Jitsudo led us in chanting the Heart Sutra, the central text of the Zen school. Among Robert's friends in the room were several serious Zen students, both lay and priest-ordained. They and I were surprised that I could remember all the words to the sutra, while they could remember none. Stress had driven the Sino-Japanese syllables out of their minds. I had always been a peripheral Zen student at best, but I had a memory for text.

Now we were in the English/Sanskrit version: "So proclaim the mantra that says Gate, Gate, Paragate, Parasamgate, Bodhi, Sva-ah . . ."

I was also oddly aware of those around me. The beautiful ICU nurse, dark-haired and dark-eyed, treated us with a courtly compassion. I told her, as she watched us sit and chant Buddhist sutras or Hebrew Psalms, "Other relatives are coming who are going to be hysterical." She was in her mid-twenties, a local Albuquerquian. When Robert's heart stopped, she wept. Later, I know she went home, to dinner, out dancing, to the movies, with a friend, a lover, or her mom. I could tell she was a very nice person and that we were a detail in her life, perhaps one she would always remember.

It was lucky Robert's family managed to arrive as quickly as they did, flying in from the East Coast. His sister Julie, who was the closest to him in age and shared history, arrived while he was still breathing on the machine. I had whispered to him, "Don't die until Julie gets here." Later Julie told me that she had seen a tear roll from Robert's bandaged eye. To me, that was just a coincidence of moisture. I had stopped believing that he could hear us. Robert's mother and his sister Suzi arrived soon after. Sobbing, they wanted explanations. The nurse caught my eye, and we allowed ourselves a smile.

"My baby," Robert's mother broke down. She had lost her only son, her first born, and her pain was palpable.

We chanted the Buddhist sutras as Robert's heart finally stopped, and he was disconnected from the respirator. He was dead.

I called one of the two mortuaries in Santa Fe, pulling out a piece of information buried somewhere in my mind that one had a good reputation for allowing unconventional customs.

Rabbi Lynn and the Zen Sensei had both cautioned us to stay with the body after Robert died. The ward secretary took this as gospel. Under religion of patient she wrote: *Stay with the body*.

I asked Jitsudo-sensei if he would perform the funeral. "But I have to pay you," I insisted.

He shook his head, offering to do it for free.

"No," I said. For years I lived with Robert, who refused to take money for the ceremonies he performed, weddings and funerals. "I need to pay you."

Jitsudo agreed.

One of Robert's friends, Bill, pulled out a razor he had brought from Santa Fe. When his girlfriend had called to tell him the situation, he had packed the razor to shave "Bobby." Bill was an ex-pro weightlifter, a tough guy out of Oklahoma turned Zen student. When Robert was his sickest, Bill had worried at me, "Bobby lies. He says he's fine, but he lies." Now Bill gave the razor to the sensei, who carefully shaved the corpse's face and head as bare as they had been the day Robert was ordained as a priest.

"I knew he would die; I knew he would die," I kept telling anyone who would listen.

I had been convinced for months that Robert would die. My friends and family were convinced this stemmed from my natural pessimism. I have a well-deserved reputation as a worrier—I come from Russian-Jewish stock, and there is a Slavic streak in my personality. Plus, I am a poet, and it is, no doubt, part of my occupation to concern myself with the fleeting nature of life. But this felt different, if only to me.

A few months before Robert died, I had a terrible dream. In it, Robert, Isabel, and I were walking down a dirt road in the summer with a group of people. A large black animal—part bear, part dog—ran out and tried to maul us. Robert fought it off. Then a farmer shot a gun, and in trying to kill the beast, he shot Robert instead. He was dead. Then came the truly upsetting part of the dream. Dead, Robert just smiled serenely. He began to pack up his orioki—three eating bowls stacked inside each other—the way I had seen him do countless times as he got ready for a stay at a Zen monastery.

In life, Robert had gone to a Zen monastery in Crestone, Colorado, every few months to spend some time or to a sit a week-long, formal meditation sesshin. He always took great care with his packing: Japanese-style black robes, warm underwear, three clean orioki bowls stacked inside each other. He even ironed the napkin, the wrapping cloths, and the chopstick envelope.

Dead, he was now packing up and preparing to leave. The thing that upset me the most in the dream was his quality of unbothered acceptance.

The day before Robert died, I had driven to Albuquerque to see him. He had post-surgical complications at that point; his stomach wasn't working, and he had a pumping tube.

For several days, he had refused to see our daughter Isabel. "I don't want her to see me like this," he said. "It might frighten her."

This was the second week of his hospitalization. My life was completely stressed. We lived sixty-five miles from the hospital, and I was grading mid-term exams for the three classes I taught at the Community College. I never even considered taking time off from work; I was the family's financial support. Isabel had just begun first grade at a small private school and was getting adjusted. Since Robert refused to see her, I couldn't visit him in the evenings. I finally took two days off from commuting to the hospital, instead sending friends to check on Robert. I felt completely torn between competing demands.

Luckily, I had gone back to Albuquerque on Thursday. Robert mostly dozed as I graded reams of remedial composition exams.

As I was leaving, he embraced me hard and batted at my breasts.

"What's that for?" I asked. I had taken his complete lack of romantic interest in me over the past months as a bad sign, an indication that the disease had the better of him.

"I don't want you to forget," he said and smiled, then added, "I never knew how much I loved you."

The sentiment gave me a chill. It felt more like a good-bye than a declaration of passion. And it was to torture me later. How could he not have known? What had he meant? Had he taken me for granted until that moment? Or was he admitting, in some obscure way, that he knew he would die, that we would be parted forever?

"I'll always love you," I said. Then I left the room.

In the parking lot, I realized I had left my address book behind. I went back—other friends were visiting—Robert smiled and waved. It was the last time I saw him alive.

In the elevator going down, I spoke with an exhausted-looking, elderly lady, whose husband was dying. "I think my husband will recover," I told her in an oddly optimistic moment. Then I added uncharacteristically, "I'll pray for you."

That night I was overwhelmed by a fear so intense I couldn't shake it. I phoned my sister long distance and told her very clearly, "Rachel, I know that Robert is going to die. Everyone thinks I'm just anxious but *I know he is going to die*. And I want someone to know that I know."

"You're so stressed Mir," she said.

But I was convinced otherwise.

"I knew he would die," I told the surgeon.

I had never liked the man. Robert and I had joked about his name, which had a built-in pun that could be construed as "Dr. Misdiagnosis." It no longer seemed funny. The surgeon had been attentive and clear with Robert, but shrugged off my questions. I figured he didn't like worried wives.

When Robert was in the coma, the surgeon had gone off-call, presumably for a weekend trip. Now, inexplicably, he was back, checking up on me. With his patient gone, he seemed willing to talk to the wife.

"People often know when a spouse is going to die," he agreed. Then he put what felt like a curse on me, "Sometimes they just drop dead themselves."

For months that haunted me. *The surgeon put the ojo—the evil eye—on me*, I thought. Indeed, I was convinced that I probably would drop dead. It was not until I visited my own GP months later that the curse was removed.

"You're not going to die," she said sharply. "Besides, the real reason you're convinced of it is that you're a single mother. When I was a single mom, I always thought the plane would crash. Besides, the surgeon was probably talking about really old people."

"I'm not going to get sick and die?" I asked.

Then she gave me a piece of priceless advice. "Keep crying," she said, "and you won't get sick and die."

But the surgeon had his compassionate side, too.

"What do I tell my daughter?" I sobbed.

He shocked me by suddenly telling me, "One of my own children died, and I had to leave the hospital and tell my other children and my first wife."

I looked at him in a new light. It was the first, but far from the last, time that people would unexpectedly reveal something of their own suffering to me.

"My office won't charge you for anything the insurance won't pay," he continued. I think he was motivated by genuine kindness, not a fear of lawsuit.

Later, at my lawyer's insistence, both an expert and I read Robert's complete medical records. We found no indication whatsoever of mismanagement or human error, for which I was grateful. Robert had trusted all his doctors and would have been appalled at a suit. And the surgeon was true to his word. His office was the only one not to dun me for bills that were as emotionally painful to receive as they were costly.

I went back to the ICU where Robert's body lay blue and cold. I bowed to it formally, having once been a Zen student myself, and took a look. That was the last time I would see him.

Fear had dogged me every day for the two years Robert had been sick. Now I wanted to be rid of my fear, a fear that had gripped me like a bad cramp in labor but that led nowhere. Like labor, the fear got worse, but there was nothing to deliver. I prayed for the sick, I prayed blindly, stupidly, and I did not expect success.

Every morning I'd wake up alone in the double bed. I'd check on my husband, hopefully asleep, on the single mattress on the floor of the room that had once been his study. He was breathing. I'd go pee. The arrangement was supposed to be temporary, that mattress. He would get well. I'd get Isabel ready for school. She'd scoot in and give him a hug. Alone in the car, I'd cry.

It was a normal enough life in some terrible way. I tried to make him well—prayer, doctors, money, massage, sex, food, jokes, planting a hedge in front of the house. I had no inner life because I was never alone. There is no imagination without solitude. I was never alone because fear buckled its seat belt beside me, fear ate off my plate, fear sipped my coffee first.

Now the fear was over, and in its place a vast psychedelic grief that sharpened some senses, dulled others, that filled my body and mind with a drug that seemed in endless supply.

Robert's sister Julie said she was going down to smoke a cigarette. I took the elevator with her. We sat in the parking lot, under a canopy of clear desert stars. I had smoked maybe five cigarettes in my life, and I needed Julie to light the cigarette for me. I held it awkwardly between my fingers, as if I were smoking a joint.

One of the nurses who had taken care of Robert, a young guy, was getting off his shift.

"How ya doin'?" he asked casually.

"Robert died," I answered.

He looked shocked. Then he said the first, but not the last, inane thing I was to hear in the months to come that was meant to condole, "Well, don't forget, he's up there looking down at ya now." He gestured to the starry sky above the parking lot.

I didn't think Robert, a Jewish Buddhist, was in some Christian heaven. The stars had never looked colder. It was hard for me to focus at all on my body's sensations. I stared at the lit end of the cigarette in an attempt to keep from floating away.

A taxicab pulled up, and my parents climbed out, looking exhausted from the trip from New Jersey.

"When did you start smoking?" my mother asked. Despite the crisis, she was acting like my mother, who had always had an abhorrence of smoking.

"Robert died, and I just started," I snapped, unable to really express my feelings.

We went back upstairs. The ICU and corridor were full of Robert's and my distraught relatives. It was at that moment I needed him the most. When our Jewish families acted up, it was Robert I depended upon for calm. *Where is he?* I kept thinking. *Where is he?* As if he had just popped out to go for a walk or was off in a corner reading a book, leaving me to cope at a dreadful party.

My father and I started to walk back and forth in the corridor.

He startled tears into my eyes by saying out of the blue, "Of everyone I ever knew, Robert was the one who best personified Emersonian self-reliance." It was an odd but accurate compliment from a sociologist to a Zen priest.

We passed the spot where the Navajo family had sat sobbing, but neither of us commented on it. I was the one sobbing now in that waiting room, catching glimpses of pity and fear from the less involved. It was going to be difficult, afterwards, to find in myself a clear account of what had happened and in what order. I had moved completely off the map of plot and into something temporarily beyond narrative.

Robert was a corpse.

The group began to split up.

I practically ordered Robert's sister Julie and Miriam B. to ride back with the body in the hearse. I was going on the directive not to leave the body alone and felt that the sister who'd adored him and a fellow Zen practitioner would be good company. It was only much later that I heard from them how difficult it had been.

Sharon said she would drive me back to Santa Fe. Like so many things in New Mexico, Robert's illness and death had involved driving through vast distances. Now my first act as a grief-stricken widow was also to start traveling.

We stopped at Sharon's boyfriend's house in the North Valley on the way home. He was the first person I saw after Robert's death who hadn't been directly involved with it. A big bear of a guy, he gave me a huge hug. Like many of the men who would later condole me, he gave me a distinct impression of *I know you are going to be all right*.

Women seemed less sure, perhaps because they identified more closely, perhaps because their worldviews depended more on love. Men, however, communicated a belief in my self-reliance, even if it was only baseless optimism on their part.

Sharon drove me back up the hill in the dark.

"What am I going to do? What am I going to do?" I asked the darkness around the car.

"Maybe you should consider getting a job, just for a while, to stabilize yourself. You know how stressful freelancing is." Sharon was a freelancer herself and practical as always.

"Like what?"

"I don't know . . . maybe with the state . . . department of tourism."

"Maybe . . . ," I said. "Or maybe I'm going to take Isabel and move to Jerusalem."

Sharon nodded.

I was all ready for extreme action. As it turned out, I never did get to the Holy Land. Instead, I was going places I had never imagined.

Smoke

We hardly slept that night. When I walked through my front door, my first impulse was to stick my head into Robert's room, as I usually did, and give him the news of the day.

"Boy, what a weird day," I wanted to say. "You died. And everyone came from New York, all the families. They were *hysterical*. I really wished you'd been there. It was horrible being alone."

Julie and I slept together in my double bed.

"I am going to get over this," I told her. "I am going to recover." I had no idea how or even what I meant, but she looked distraught.

"I am never going to get over this," she said.

This difference in attitude was a gulf that would come to divide me from Robert's family for quite some time. All I knew was that some survival mechanism deep inside me, which I hadn't known existed, kicked in the night Robert died. You could call it instinct or life force, and it was so powerful that eventually I began to call it God.

My first inkling that I would survive was that I kept hearing in my head the phrase, *I don't want this to be the last thing that happens to me.*

It wasn't that I didn't long for death many times in the following weeks. Hope even worried I was suicidal and offered to remove sharp implements from my kitchen.

On a superficial level, it was my responsibility to Isabel that kept me going. But on a much deeper level, it was an impersonal force.

Robert and I had often had semi-serious disagreements about how we would have managed in a Nazi concentration camp. I was haunted by those events in Jewish history that had occurred right before I was born and had fantasized since childhood about if I would or would not have survived. Robert, with the New Jersey punk side of his nature ascendant over the Zen priest, was always a proponent of shooting one's way out.

I would agree, but then he would mock me, "Why even worry? You'd never have even made it to a concentration camp. You'd have died on the train."

He'd seen me in everyday life often flattened by hunger, fatigue, or demands. He thought of himself as the tough one. Now he was dead at thirty-six, removed from all dilemmas, real and imagined, moral or otherwise.

I was alive and angry. *You fucker,* I thought. *I didn't die on the train. I'm still here and fighting, even if you're not.*

I woke up screaming Robert's name several times. Julie saw his figure floating beyond the kitchen window in the darkened backyard. Sharon, sleeping on the living room couch, heard crashing and bumping throughout the night.

In the morning Sharon bleakly said, "If I never spend another night like that again, it will be too soon."

My gray alley cat, Cassandra, had died just a few weeks before, right before Yom Kippur. She was almost twenty years old, a ferocious fighter who had had an infected wound from a cat fight only a few months before she died. Scrappy as she was, she died peacefully on the lintel of the bathroom door, a place she had favored for snoozing. Even though she had been unusually long-lived for a cat, it had not seemed like a good sign.

Robert had often been her rescuer, taking her down from high walls behind our San Francisco flat, looking for her in snowstorms in Santa Fe. He had always promised me that he would give her a resplendent formal Buddhist funeral, complete with incense and gongs.

When she died, he was too sick to get out of bed.

I wrapped Cassandra in my favorite scarf, and a friend, Russell, who also did some gardening for us, buried her beneath a rose bush. Robert and Isabel and I sat around and reminisced about our cat's many adventures, her feisty personality, her more-than-nine lives. I was content, but apparently Robert was not.

Right before his surgery, he called his sister Julie to say that if he died *he* wanted a formal Buddhist funeral. He complained that I had not properly honored the cat. He had told me as well that he wanted the funeral of a Buddhist priest, but apparently he did not trust me to do it. All he would say about it, half jokingly, was that such a ceremony would be very complicated and very expensive.

After the cat died, Robert had remarked that various noises around the house he had blamed on her had continued. I had blamed Robert's nocturnal wanderings, his insomnia, and diarrhea for the creaks and groans of our old house. Now both the cat and Robert were gone, and the house seemed noisier than ever, full of restless ghosts.

Even if we hadn't really slept, we awoke bursting with adrenaline. Sharon and I wrote the obituary; it seemed natural, as freelance writers, for that to be our first task.

"What shall we say instead of flowers?" Sharon asked.

I set up a fund at the public library, where Robert had worked for years. I sat in my living room and made decisions. Meanwhile, the room seemed oddly bright one moment, then dark the next. Shadows coiled in corners, the furniture shimmered like the start of a bad-acid trip. My senses were deranged, it was hard to stand, I couldn't eat, I pissed, and my urine was dark and dank, smelling of bile.

Then my daughter came through the door with Hope.

Many years later, Isabel would say, "It must have been hard for Hope that night, smiling all that time, knowing Dad was dead."

Hope said that wasn't the hard part. The hard part was bringing Isabel in the next morning, knowing *little girl, your life is about to change forever*. Hope said it was the hardest thing she had ever had to do. It was the hardest thing I ever had to do as well, and I wanted to get it over with as fast as possible.

"Isabel," I said. "Dad died."

She gave a sob, a shriek, then settled into steady dreadful tears. My daughter was six years old, and she seemed to get it, all the way through the cells of her small body. Her father was dead. He was gone. And he wasn't coming back.

In the months after Robert's death, I sat in grief groups, often listening to grown adults recount losses of twenty, thirty, or more years ago. As children, they had been denied their grief. There is a truism that children can't grieve, that they don't "understand" death, as if adults did.

Someone asked my sister Rachel, known for her snappy wit, if Isabel "understood" Robert's death.

Rachel retorted, "You mean, does she understand how a person could be here one minute and then gone forever the next? Does she know where he went? How this happened? Frankly, *I* don't understand. Do you?"

Isabel was allowed to grieve. She wasn't told to cheer up, that Daddy was fine in heaven, and most of all, she wasn't told to take care of Mommy.

But that didn't mean the process wasn't terrifying to me. My child was distraught almost to the point of dissociation, and there was nothing I could do except listen, hold her, and listen.

It was fortunate that from Saturday morning on, twelve hours after Robert died, we were descended upon by literally dozens of other people—friends, family, and community. For the next three or four days, there was usually an average of forty people in our small stucco house. They bathed Isabel, fed her, read to her, took her to the movies, and sat with her. Her friends came, as well, because it appears that, left alone, children can condole, as well as grieve.

Talaya, a contemporary of Isabel's and the daughter of old friends of Robert's, wrote a condolence note that said it all. "I am sorry that your father and husband died. Love, Talaya."

Reuben, Hope's oldest son, seared himself on Isabel's memory by his appearance in a never-before-or-after-seen tie and jacket at the memorial service. But he impressed his mother and me by apparently musing for days over death and then concluding, "Well, Robert is with Mozart and Beethoven." Robert would have been amused, even though as the long-time member of several rock bands, he probably would have preferred to be with Jimi Hendrix.

It seemed as if everyone I knew in New Mexico was crammed into my house.

Actually, the Zen students were busy sitting with Robert's corpse. His body was in the funeral home, and his friends had set it up with the director so that they could sit in cross-legged meditation with him twenty-four hours a day until the body was cremated. My friend Russell, who had buried my cat, was now sitting zazen next to Robert's corpse. The Zen students took the directive not to leave Robert's corpse alone very seriously.

Miriam B. floated between the funeral home and the house, saying it was strange, but the men were with Robert and the women were with me.

For the first few days after Robert's death, women surrounded me, and a lone man looked awkward entering my house. The women took over. One arranged poignant photographs of Robert as a young man on the mantle. One took all my dirty sheets, towels, and laundry to her house—even though I have a washing machine—washed, dried, and returned it.

The food began arriving; former Midwesterners brought scalloped potatoes while New Mexicans brought steaming trays of enchiladas. There were chicken soup, posole, and a lot of chocolate. I ate none of this food, and months later had to throw out casseroles with freezer burn, but it was good the food was there because now dozens of people needed to be fed.

Along with the food came flowers, not from locals but far-flung relatives. Robert's sister Suzi, who was blonde and extremely beautiful in a Juliette of the Spirits way, had numerous admirers who sent gifts and flowers. The one that made me saddest was an enormous white floral arrangement from my favorite of her exes, an Italian guy from New Jersey I'd always loved. Because we came out of the same cultural milieu, those white gladioli said "death" to me the way nothing else had.

Robert's obituary had gone on the Internet, and the phone was ringing off the hook with his childhood friends, a small press network he knew as the publisher of a literary magazine, people in New York and California.

My own siblings arrived. Rachel had left her two small children for the first time because I had insisted that Steve, her husband, come too, as he had been a particular favorite of Robert's. My youngest sister Susannah arrived with husband, a toddler, and baby in tow; in her family no one went anywhere alone. My brother Daniel, ten years younger than I, came with his wife Alisa. I heard later about the dreadfully bumpy landing their plane made into the Albuquerque airport. Steve, who was given to motion sickness, even vomited. Everyone else was terrified until Rachel announced with authority, "This plane will not crash. God would not do that to our mother."

It was Saturday night. Robert's memorial was Monday; he was cremated Tuesday morning. The three and a half days between his death and cremation were among the strangest in my life. I seemed to be at the heart of a vortex, which, like a black hole, pulled past, present, and future together simultaneously.

The phone rang. It was my best friend Kath, an inveterate traveler through exotic locales, calling from Seoul, Korea, where she was teaching English. She was getting on a plane, she explained clearly, to come to drive me and Isabel to the funeral. Kath was one of the few people I knew who had truly been a friend of the family's, close in different but intense ways to all three of us. She always relied on Robert for romantic advice in her tempestuous love affairs. She'd taken care of Isabel when she was a baby and given this small girl a taste for exotic adventure, inspired in part by Kath's dashboard collection of silk flowers from China.

When I got off the phone, everything went black for a moment, and I fell to the wooden kitchen floor. Kath was coming. Things were better, and worse, than I'd expected. One of the people I loved most in the world was about to travel thousands of miles to be with me. On the other hand, this meant that Robert was truly dead.

Saturday night there was a strange party in my kitchen. About a dozen women showed up, all drinking and smoking cigarettes. Sharon had gotten a friend to bring a huge bottle of sherry wine and had procured her own drug of choice: an enormous bottle of Advil, as though we were facing some gigantic communal migraine. Hope sat in one of my straight-backed kitchen chairs, watching her daughter Pearl, who had just learned to walk. Hope told me later that she felt curiously protected by Pearl's presence, as if being the only mother of a young child in my kitchen, she was somehow temporarily exempt from suffering.

Someone had discovered Robert's stash of strong Sherman cigarettes, and we began to smoke them. Old friends of mine, a long-standing couple, were there, and one picked up a Sherman's and inhaled with delight. She'd quit smoking twenty years before, but it now seemed like a good time to start. Her girlfriend was totally horrified, got up and sat on a banco in the living room to fan away the smoke. This little scene was repeated the next day when a friend, who usually had a cool, elegant appearance, her black hair pinned up in braids, suddenly toked up on a joint.

Her husband, who had only known her for fifteen years, sputtered: "You don't smoke dope!"

"I do now," she replied calmly, inhaling.

Smokables were everywhere. As a rule, I did not do drugs. When I was young, they made me disoriented and queasy. As a pregnant woman and nursing mother, I barely drank coffee. I was also pretty much of a teetotaler.

However, in this crisis, anodynes had never looked so good. I was also given two large blue Valiums, which I regarded as kind of emergency suicide pills, but I never used them. And as a sign of the times, I was also offered—one—Prozac. Even in my grief-stricken state, I found this faintly hilarious. Prozac and its cousins, of course, take weeks to work, but it was the sign of an ex-druggie simply to offer whatever drugs were on hand.

There were many parties all weekend, small private parties of grief, little parties of sex and breaking up, of adultery and reconciliation. I heard a great deal of gossip later. Robert's death produced a wake of a hundred baby boomers doing what they traditionally did in a crisis: flirting, getting stoned, talking about each other. I might have been back in high school.

Kath showed up, looking dazed after flying sixteen hours from Asia for the sole purpose of driving me to my husband's funeral. Isabel flew into Kath's arms, confirming for us all that Kath had done the right thing. When she walked in the door, it was as if for a moment nothing had changed—my husband was alive, my best friend was in town, and we were going to get some take-out Chinese food to eat it in the backyard.

In her hand Kath had a fat strand of bodhi beads, those Buddhist rosaries or malas, which she'd bought for Robert at a temple in Seoul. Now she delivered them, but to a corpse. I put out my hand, and she gave the string to me. Each bead was smooth and round, larger than a walnut. As actual rosaries, these strands were no longer used to count prayers; it was the fashion among Zen students to wear them twisted around a wrist as a kind of identity and mindfulness practice. Robert had worn his continually, and he would have liked a strand from a Buddhist country.

The night Robert died, there were about fifteen people in the ICU. But no one could find Robert's mala, the bodhi beads he'd worn on his wrist for fourteen years. A cheap watch, yes, an address book, a clip-on fan, and a book about adventures at sea, but no beads.

"Does anyone have a mala?" Jitsudo-sensei asked, and like a scene in a western where everyone pulls a gun from his pocket, a half dozen people pulled beads off their wrists, out of handbags, off their necks. Jitsudo wrapped a strand around Robert's wrist.

Kath borrowed a truck and showed up on Monday to drive Isabel and me up Cerro Gordo Canyon to the small Buddhist temple where Robert's memorial service would be held. According to his only request, he would have all the Buddhist ceremonies associated with a Zen priest.

The temple was actually a Tibetan stupa that had been set out in traditional fashion. Robert often pointed out that it had the necessary hill shaped like a turtle to the north and running water, the Santa Fe River, to the south. The central stupa, or pagoda, housed reams of prayers. Robert had also been delighted when he'd discovered that the prayers had been copied at the local copy shop instead of written out by hand, which apparently was equally kosher.

Adobe walls surrounded the stupa, and a small meditation hall, arranged in traditional zendo style, had been Robert's home temple for years. The stupa had been given as a gift to Richard Baker-roshi, and Robert had practiced there since we had moved to Santa Fe in 1984. It was the only appropriate place for his funeral.

Jitsudo-sensei officiated at the ceremony. Once again, his presence was calming and focused; he was literally a lifesaver in this situation.

Jitsudo had told me before the ceremony, "Your husband felt free to go because he knew you would take care of everything." His words both reassured me and made me angry. Of course, I would take care of everything. Hadn't I supported us, raised Isabel, kept house, cared for Robert when he was sick, been the fiscally responsible one, the practical one? And I knew he had secretly scorned me for it, regarding me as earthbound and materialistic, while he felt free to pursue the role of the unattached monk. And so, yes, now that he was gone, I would continue to take care of everything. There was nothing new about that.

We had once had a mundane marital argument about something like health insurance. I had proclaimed, "Money is security." Robert had found this so hilarious that he had actually fallen on the floor laughing. Although he was a Zen priest, our roles were, to some extent, traditionally Jewish ones. He was the spiritual one, like a rabbi unburdened by practical concerns. I was a classic rabbi's wife, a rebettzin, running a chicken farm, or the equivalent, to make ends meet.

We had set up an altar with Robert's photograph—a black-and-white enlargement of a color snapshot my mother had taken several years before. In it, he was plump and smiling, head shaved, wearing a favorite red T-shirt. Oddly, he was repairing a doll of Isabel's whose head had snapped off. In the photograph, handy as always, he was carefully wiring the doll's head back to its body.

On the altar was also a pair of Robert's blue plastic flip-flops, which he wore like Japanese-style zoris beneath his priest's robes. The altar also displayed his raksu, a ritual bib with his Buddhist name, written in calligraphy, which meant Blue/Green Willow Watercourse, a wooden memorial tablet with his name, and the three orioki bowls I had seen in my dream before his death. The altar was set beneath the portal of the small temple.

Several hundred people were crammed—standing—into the circular courtyard around the stupa.

Jisudo led the ceremony with grace and concentration. It was similar to all the other Zen ceremonies I had ever seen, from ordinations to weddings, in that it involved bowing, full prostration, the offering of incense, chanting the Heart Sutra. In many ways, it was eerily similar to our wedding.

Because it was a funeral, it also involved the offering of bowls of sticky rice to the deceased. I asked everyone who had been in the ICU with Robert to come and offer incense.

I spent the service standing alone, yet near a cluster of friends.

Isabel had finally refused to come into the temple. My father took her to play in the adjacent park, seemingly relieved to be out of the context of weird Eastern religion once and for all and able to do something he understood as useful.

I was wearing my favorite dark green skirt and vest of a watered rayon material. I should not have chosen them, because

I later felt compelled to throw them out, as if they were contaminated. The same thing happened to the dress I wore the next day to the cremation. I also wore one of Robert's coats, one I had always coveted. It was a hundred-year-old, Chinese merchant's coat he'd bought on Manhattan's lower East Side, made of exquisite, light-weight, striped, blue wool with buttoning frogs. I later gave the coat away, as well, much as I loved it, to an old friend of Robert's, who was about to receive an important lineage ordination and was sewing her robes out of material that had belonged to dead people. I imagined she cut it up, and although I had always wanted the coat—indeed, even begged Robert to let me borrow it on special occasions—in the end, I could not possess it.

It was a beautiful autumn day. Northern New Mexico was ablaze with yellow and purple flowers, its classic chamisa and asters. The sky was an arch of piercing turquoise. Weeks of lovely balmy weather lay ahead. We did not have our usual early alpine snows. That weather kept me going; no matter how distraught I felt, at least it wasn't dark and cold.

People spoke affectionately of Robert at the service.

Then the poetry began. At first, there were some stunning ones by real poets. Robert and I knew many writers, and they turned out to honor him. But the poems kept going and going. I began to fear the rustle of paper pulled from the sentimental pocket of some amateur, who would momentarily be reading a mediocre verse about death, as I was forced to listen.

Eventually, I spoke up and invited everyone back to my house for the reception. My mother had catered huge platters of vegetables, meat, and fruit from Albertson's grocery store.

At least a hundred people crowded into my small house and spread out into the backyard. Old friends had arrived earlier, unasked, with dozens of rental chairs and tables for everyone.

In my bedroom, my first cousin Alex was setting up to say Kaddish. Temporarily, we were Jews instead of Buddhists. During the period of mourning, I would switch back and forth between religions. It wasn't even confusing; I could use all the help I could get. Alex handed out copied sheets of the prayer. About forty Jews crammed into the room.

Renée, who was Italian, was still grieving her old boyfriend Bill Gersh, a Taos painter, who despite his wild-man ways, was often called a Jewish Mother.

"Bill always said I was Jewish by insemination," she said, sobbing at the joke. Renée came in and said Kaddish, too.

My experience with the prayer had been limited up to this point. I had been raised an atheist without any formal Jewish education. My Jewish interest in my late thirties led me to study Hebrew and to join the local synagogue, but my ability to read Hebrew was minimal and even less so my Aramaic, the language of Kaddish. Both my parents were living, and I had never recited it for a relative. In fact, I had only said it once before and then under very sad circumstances.

Among the group of women in Santa Fe who were friends and writers was Patty, who had converted to Judaism when she married a Jew. She and her husband had two children, and then the marriage broke up, in part because of his new insistence on orthodoxy and criticism of her as "not being a real Jew."

I remembered her, though, lighting Sabbath candles and baking challah. She began to drink so heavily that a few of us ran an intervention on her and begged her to go into rehab. She never stayed on the wagon for long. I'd see her around town, at poetry readings, drunk and bloated, but always retaining some of her sweetness.

A few years later she died, a tragic death, drowning drunk in the bathtub in a cheap motel outside of Las Vegas, New Mexico. Her family was completely estranged from her. I don't know if they even attended the funeral.

An old friend held a small memorial service in a living room for Patty. Her country neighbors came, mostly old-fashioned Spanish people who had loved her warmth, while knowing her troubles. Three Jewish writers also came, including me. Robert had just fallen gravely ill, and it seemed like the right thing to do. We stumbled over Kaddish together, reading out of a prayer book. We had no minyan, the quorum of Jews necessary to say the prayer. But it felt the least we could do for a woman who had been as much a practitioner of Judaism as we. Then the neighbors said the Lord's Prayer. We reminisced and went home.

My acquaintance with Kaddish had now begun in earnest, though. Although the opening words brought tears to my eyes— and echoes of Allen Ginsberg's poem, as well as the Kaddish recitation in "Schindler's List"—the prayer itself irritated me. It didn't say anything consoling about grief, my grief, or that mourners should be comforted, or the dead remembered, or anything useful. It would take me a while to penetrate the use of the words, "May the name of the Lord be exalted; May the name of the Lord be sanctified." It was as if they purposively took me away from myself. It wasn't my grief that was important at that moment, but to turn and concentrate on the Divine.

Out in the backyard, people were eating strawberries and melon slices. Some musician friends of Robert's had a small gamelan orchestra playing. As with any group composed heavily of artists and writers, people were conducting a bit of business, talking to each other, networking. Someone later complained she felt it desecrated the situation, but I was from a New York City garment-industry family, after all, where business was conducted readily at weddings, bar mitzvahs, and funerals.

I finally got into bed and went to sleep in the middle of the reception.

When I awoke, people were cleaning up. Someone with a truck volunteered to take all the trash to the dump.

Someone else's husband gave me a neck rub and brushed my breasts, seemingly inadvertently. But I could sense the intention, and it was becoming clearer to me: I was a woman alone, a widow, and perhaps, fair game.

That night, missing the memorial service but just in time for the cremation, my best friend from high school, Juliet, arrived. She had tawny hair, an enviable figure, an earthy manner, and I adored her. An actor's manager in Los Angeles, she still had New York manners, a mix of toughness and chic. Her familiar appearance made me feel safer, much as Kath's had.

Kath and Juliet were also glad to see each other. They'd met once before, and Juliet, immediately taken with Kath's sultry but underutilized looks, had made her up with eye shadow and lipstick until she looked like Frida Kahlo on a good day.

Juliet was also my clothes consultant for my cremation outfit.

"What should I wear?" I asked stupidly, as if we were going to a party.

"What do you want to be?" Juliet asked. It didn't bother her that I'd asked such an inappropriate question. After all, we'd been talking about clothes our whole lives.

"A widow," I said. Then I added, "Now that I'm single, should I lose ten pounds?"

"Fifteen," Juliet pronounced.

The next morning Kath drove me to Berardinelli Mortuary. In the truck I said, "Juliet says that now I'm single, I need to lose fifteen pounds."

"Juliet is from L.A.," said Kath. "I think you should just go for ten."

We walked into the blue hushed chapel and started laughing so hard we had to hold on to each other to keep from falling over. To begin with, Kath could not believe that she, who was half-Italian and half-Jewish, was suddenly in a classic Italian mortuary. She was having flashbacks to a previous life where she had worn black and had started wailing and couldn't stop. We also were laughing because Robert's body was in a box. A very large box, which cost much less than a casket, but still one that looked alarming like the many cartons Robert used to ship UPS.

"Robert LOVED boxes," said Kath.

"Oh, God, he loved boxes," I agreed.

"Robert would have liked this," Kath said. "He would have liked this whole scene—him in a box, dead, you and me hysterical in an Italian mortuary."

I started sobbing and had to clutch her once more.

Robert's body in the box was placed in the crematorium, which was located in what felt like a suburban garage. About forty people were gathered for another formal Buddhist ceremony. Russell was there to officiate in a Zen capacity. We again offered incense and chanted.

Then Russ pushed the large red button that started the cremation process. Only a few members of the family were there, my brother, his wife, one of Robert's sisters and myself. The rest of the families obviously could not handle this visceral confrontation with his death. Julie, Robert's sister, trembled violently as she tried to light an incense stick, hands shaking. But oddly, although the people there were somewhat randomly self-selected, someone was there from almost every community Robert had been involved with.

After the crematorium was fired up, the funeral director told us it would take three hours for the body to burn. We could come back at the end, but even then the ashes wouldn't be cooled and ready until the next day.

My friend the poet, Joan Logghe, announced that she was off to teach her writing class on grief in the AIDS community; anyone was welcome. Like the gamelan concert after the memorial service, Robert would have enjoyed arts events that somehow were interspersed with his death.

Kath, Juliet, and I went out into the parking lot. Looking back at the funeral parlor, we could see a heat wave rising out of the chimney of the crematorium.

"Take a good look," Kath said. "In case you want to remember this. Take a good look. Look, there are telephone wires. Birds." She spoke as if to a child.

"Kathleen," I told her, "I'm sorry. I'm sorry you had to go through this. I'm so glad you came, but I know you hate this."

She nodded.

Juliet stood stock still in the October sunshine. I touched her shoulder; her hair gleamed.

I said, "But I'm not going to apologize to you, Juliet. I know you're chalking this up to experience. This is part of a story: The husband of my best friend from high school, who was a Zen priest, died when he was thirty-six, and I went to the cremation."

"You're right," she said. We were laughing again in the parking lot of the Italian mortuary.

As Robert's body burned, Juliet took me out for sushi. It was odd, because it was the last meal I could eat in public for many weeks. I felt too raw and vulnerable to eat in public, and besides, eating just didn't interest me. Yet, in her company, sitting in a little room made of tatami mats in Robert's favorite restaurant in town, I almost could taste the food.

The next day, Miriam B. and I went to pick up the ashes, which were given to me in yet another box, a small one of heavy gray plastic. Of course, I opened the box immediately and saw what I'd expected: two pounds of coarse gray ash mixed with chips of bone. Miriam drove the bumpy, partially paved road up

Cerro Gordo Canyon while I balanced the box in my lap. We were taking the ashes back to the Zen temple, where they would rest for forty-nine days, the traditional Buddhist period of mourning.

I was seized with a desire to open the ashes and sprinkle a handful in the little park outside the temple, but they were securely tied in a clear plastic bag, and I didn't have a knife. Robert had always hated the way I opened packages or food containers; I just tore and ripped and hacked. He was always conscientious in the way he respectfully handled physical objects. And I heard his voice in my head, reprimanding me as I contemplated tearing the plastic open. So I left it untouched.

From the Buddhist viewpoint, the cremation was as final as a burial. Still, there was the matter of the ashes. Many people wanted a little bit of Robert to scatter on their own land or to keep in a medicine pouch. Miriam B. kindly took on the slightly grisly task of dividing up the ashes. She spread newspapers on the floor and parceled bits of ash into containers.

Eventually, the rest came back to me.

A week later, cleaning out Robert's room, I turned over a box and out fell his mala, his bodhi beads, the Tibetan bone ones from Cost Plus in San Francisco that he'd restrung on cat gut so they'd be stronger. He must have taken them off before his hospitalization and inadvertently saved them from going up in smoke.

Bardo

"Last night I dreamed that you weren't dead
We'd broken up
You were still sick, but well enough
To hold a job
I yelled at you on the phone: "why the hell
Can't you come home once in a while
And read your daughter a good-night story?"

"I Know Who You Are" from *The Widow's Coat*

Different periods of mourning were allocated to me by the Jewish and Buddhist religions. I decided to observe shiva, the traditional eight days of Jewish mourning. During that time, I would not go back to work, but instead stay in my house and receive condolence calls. I would not act like a hostess, serving guests, but rather let them serve me as the bereaved.

Isabel had tried to go back to school the day of Robert's cremation, but had soon called sobbing, needing to come home.

"My brain doesn't work," she cried.

I felt much the same way.

I mostly lay on the stained gray couch in my living room. It seemed to be a truism from the books I soon started to read about being widowed; that the days after the funeral were the hardest, when everyone had gone home.

In my case, it seemed as if no one ever went home. True, Juliet had returned to Los Angeles, and Kath to Korea, and my family back to their various locales. But my friends continued to care for Isabel and me. A far-flung network of old friends had just begun to mobilize their visits, my father came back ten days later to check on us, and my sister Rachel and my brother Daniel soon followed.

I also now had my Kaddish minyan. A woman, who was a para-rabbinic at the synagogue, organized ten Jews to show up at my house every afternoon. It was an odd group. The minyan was mostly conventional, Reform Jews, whom I was sure were looking askance at my generally eclectic decor. No wall-to-wall carpeting, instead a mouse hole in the wooden floor patched with the top of a tin can. No brass trays from Israel, just a scary mask from Mexico of a bearded man's face superimposed on a toad's body. My furniture was old and worn and had been used as the cat's scratching post. The paint in the bathroom was peeling, as were the ugly linoleum tiles I had always meant to replace. Still, the minyan showed up and prayed.

And I was happy to see a therapist and attorney I knew personally from town in the minyan. But despite best efforts, we were often short several people. However, there were usually a few lackadaisical Jews, lurking about my kitchen, who would come into the living room and be counted.

A journalist friend, who had been very fond of Robert, came regularly, saying, "All this Buddhism felt too cold. I need some Judeo-Christianity."

But my back-neighbor Marie was the most faithful minyan member, despite being raised Catholic in Texas; she attended and prayed every day. In an unconventional move, she was counted as a full member.

Shiva lasts eight days, and so it is always interrupted by the observance of Shabbos. It is forbidden to mourn on the Sabbath—Kaddish isn't said—and the mourner gets a tiny preview of a return to life, no matter how frightening.

My friends made a huge Sabbath dinner, and once again my house flowed with women. We ate chicken and potatoes and lit the candles. Mostly writers and poets, they flowed through the house in their chiffon dresses and silver jewelry.

"This is the nicest Shabbos I've ever had," said a friend, who then blanched at her mistake.

"This is the worst I've ever had," I said. My husband had been dead a week.

Still, I understood what she meant. We were united as friends, and the candles had never shone brighter.

Shabbos helped me also to get through the first of many anniversaries. The first week's anniversary of Robert's death. On the last day of shiva, it is traditional for the bereaved finally to stand with the others to pray, another marker of the passage of time. I did stand, and it was a powerful spiritual moment, despite the fact that it was taking place while I was wearing sweatpants and in my own living room.

The Jewish period of strict mourning was over, yet barely ten days had passed since Robert's death. In total, traditional Judaism gave me thirty days of mourning for a spouse; Buddhism gave me forty-nine.

I went back to work, teaching at the Community College. Isabel was at school, but I tried to call my phone machine every hour, because she would often call sobbing.

I put her into art therapy immediately with a kindly therapist used to working with children. Isabel began to build large doll-sized sculptures of her father. They were highly realistic; she used a tennis ball for his bald head. In one, he sat cross-legged in black monk's robes. In another, he wore a familiar outfit of a red shirt and blue pants, the same outfit he wore in the memorial photograph on the altar. Isabel had the original framed by her bed.

Isabel had just entered first grade at a cozy alternative school. She seemed completely disoriented. The principal and teachers were extraordinarily kind and attentive, even consulting a grief therapist to get some advice on helping her.

But it was an uphill road. Normally, an enthusiastic but stubborn child, she now sobbed at slight frustrations, fought with her friends, and even threw a chair. At home, it seemed we fought constantly. She was sleeping in the same bed as I was, in part because I was too tired by the end of the day for a going-to-bed battle. I felt like a failure as a mother, but it was also comforting to feel her small warm person next to me. Besides, I was ready for bed myself by eight o'clock.

The rabbi at our synagogue phoned to check on us, and I went to see him. In a small comedy of errors, he had assumed I was not a member of his congregation (I had joined the summer before but was not on any list), and he was then chagrined he hadn't paid a formal condolence call. I, never having been a synagogue member before, had been very touched that he had called at all, more so when I discovered it hadn't originally been out of formal obligation.

Sitting in his office, I asked his advice. He suggested that Isabel start religious school on Sundays, which turned out to be very helpful, because it began to give her a spiritual context in which she could experience her grief. His advice to me was less helpful; he suggested I stay in a mourning period for a year, as one might for a parent. This was not traditional; orthodoxy gave me thirty days.

I walked out into the parking lot, musing. A Reform rabbi, trying to meet a mourner's emotional needs, suggested a year. But I decided to stick with tradition. There must be some reason for its shortness.

I thought suddenly about young widows on the lower East Side of Manhattan, probably with lots of children, money worries . . . wouldn't they want to marry again and soon? Armed with an image of a tough immigrant widow, I decided to do what she would have done; thirty days (or forty-nine, at most) was enough for me. During that time, I decided, I would take no hallucinogenic drugs or sleep with any new lovers, not that I usually did those things. I also would not cut my hair.

Back at the Community College, I had to confront my classes, which were about midway through the semester and chafing from a series of substitutes. I knew they needed me, if only to pass freshman composition. I had one small evening class that was composed mostly of returnee students with old-fashioned values. They were Pueblo Indian, Jewish, Hispanic, and Irish, all from different places, but with the same seriousness about education.

The night I returned, a spokeswoman handed me a bundle of cash neatly tied with a red ribbon. It was to help with the funeral expenses.

"Please, don't try and return it," they insisted.

Then the youngest member of the class piped up, "We put it into two-dollar bills to make it fancy so you wouldn't give it back."

At home I finally counted it: $64. I decided to spend it all on myself, went to Kaune's, the local gourmet grocery store, and bought wrinkled black olives, green olives stuffed with almonds, capers, pickled eggplant, and pimentos. My composition class, with their gesture, had helped bring back my appetite for something spicy.

The students in my composition class were not the only traditional people to help me. I had always loved my neighbors, who were essentially one sprawling family, who owned four lots, two on each side of us. They were old-fashioned people, boasting the last name of a famous Spanish explorer. Grace was the matriarch, a small bent woman who had been widowed years ago. Her grown sons lived in the compound around her, along with her eldest daughter who was a grandmother.

The first time I was ever on this block on the unfashionable west side, it was because the realtor had taken me into a neighborhood I could afford. It was a block of barking dogs, guys working on diesel trucks, and quiet stucco and adobe houses, walled from the street. When I first walked up to number 626, I fell in love, despite the crumbling steps and the paint being the color of old blood. The house was spacious, shady, peaceful, and it reminded me, for no discernible reason, of my grandparents' house on Lantana Avenue in New Jersey. It was home.

I grew to be on friendly terms with my neighbors, but any wall between us literally came down when I hired my brother to build me a small studio in the backyard. The city at first refused us a permit, because of a disputed boundary line. The line of the wall—the assumed mutual boundary—was at odds with the survey. I owned about ten inches of what we'd thought was Grace's land, and the city insisted I claim it to build legally.

My brother knocked a hole in the wall to begin building. Everyone in Grace's family measured our yard: the son from faraway Arizona and the daughter who worked for the state. I offered iced tea; they admired my house. Grace gave permission to build on the disputed area.

But it was only the day that my brother began to dig the foundation by hand that I realized what good neighbors I had. Grace's son-in-law, Norberto, appeared, driving a backhoe. He gestured dramatically to my brother to stand back. Then, in a quarter of an hour, he dug out the foundation, a thousand-dollars-worth of labor, and backed away, smiling.

After Robert died, members of the extended family stopped me in the street, as they always had, but not to chat about the weather or the growing worth of our real estate. Now they offered sympathy in their own way.

At the end of my driveway, Norberto pronounced, "Life goes on." Then, to my surprise, he produced a business card for his machine shop and said, "If you hear a noise, anything worries you, call us any hour of the day or night."

I knew that any hapless burglar in my backyard would be set upon by an armed contingent of neighbors, and I slept more easily.

It was Grace who left the angel, crocheted of white and silver yarn, tied to our doorknob for our daughter, along with some bubble bath.

The eldest son said simply, "Your husband didn't look that ill. He was always waving."

My neighbors did not attempt to rationalize or even understand death. They simply accepted it. But I sometimes thought about what Norberto had said. He was old enough to be my grandfather, was a beat-up, weathered guy. Yet somehow, I believed him.

When Robert died, I was confronted with the fact that many of our contemporaries had little experience with death. And many of them were terrified of saying the wrong thing to me or simply did not know what to say.

Months after Robert had died, I ran into an acquaintance who looked none too pleased to see me. "I wanted to say the right thing, the perfect spiritual thing," he said, "but since I couldn't figure out what it was, I just didn't call."

Numerous people asked me if I was financially secure, planning to move, or selling my house. Since these people were neither my accountant nor my realtor, and most particularly people I would never discuss my financial affairs with normally, the inquiry felt rude and invasive.

Over and over, people also told me I looked well. I was horrified that they were judging my looks during a crisis. I also felt an implied criticism here, as if my friends were actually surprised I hadn't lost my looks in one fell swoop. I eventually realized people were probably saying they were relieved to see me. It would have been easier to have them say that.

The most startling attempt at condolence came from my mother-in-law, who had told me at the funeral, "I hope you will remarry." Although I later chalked this up to her distraught mental state, in time I grew oddly grateful to her for the thought.

Strangely enough, it was the UPS deliveryman who said something I will always cherish. Robert had had several home businesses and used UPS a lot. The deliveryman expressed shock over his death and then said simply, "Your husband was a very nice man, who was always smiling." That meant a lot to me.

I also appreciated memories of any sort that people shared with me, even lighthearted ones, such as the ones about Robert always being a great source of juicy gossip and an inspiration to stop going to boring dinner parties.

After Robert died, books were dedicated to him, money was given in his memory, and a faralito with his name on it was lit in a Hospice event on Santa Fe's Plaza.

But, of all the things done in his memory, the best and oddest was done by an old acquaintance, Jessie. She had been our back neighbor at our first apartment in Santa Fe, and we had always liked each other but had never been close friends. Jessie heard through the grapevine of Robert's death. She went into her yard to look up at the stars for solace. Then she again heard the barking and whimpering of the neighbor's mistreated dog. Jessie had complained to the neighbors several times about how they mistreated the animal, but to no avail. Then Jessie thought about Robert, who had always loved animals. His untimely death reminded her that life is short. Jessie decided to act. She untied the dog, put him in her car, and drove fifty miles to friends of hers who had a ranch in the mountains. She presented them with the dog. They accepted, and the dog has a new and happy life. Months later, she told me this story, saying she had dedicated the canine rescue to Robert.

I was very cheered and amused by stories my friends told me about widows they knew who had bounced back. Ana made me laugh at my own husband's funeral. She told me a story about her aunt on the border. Her aunt was fortyish when her husband died. He was a lawyer, owned a building, and left the aunt, his wife, some money. After his death, she visited his grave each Sunday. Ana's mother would drive the aunt to the cemetery. The aunt wore her black lace mantilla over her long hair that was braided tightly and pinned in a high bun. Her wrists smelled like the rosewater she dabbed on from a blue cobalt bottle, the exact shade of the desert sky turning from blue to night at 5:45 on a winter's afternoon in Nogales. She dabbed rosewater behind her pretty ears and on her ample cleavage, and then she threw her-self down on the grave. Ana's mother could hear everything she said. The aunt would pray violently for a moment, cross herself, and fall to her knees. Her black mantilla would swing like a curtain between worlds.

She'd say, "While you were alive, I never prospered. Why did you let those rents go? Do you have any idea what that property is worth? Well, listen."

She'd recite, like a ledger book, what she was getting for each property. What she had bought and what she had sold. Securities, silver, bonds, she listed her worth to her dead husband.

Ana made me laugh. She threw herself down in my backyard, imitating her aunt.

"Did she ever remarry?" I wanted to know.

"No, she just made money. She died a rich woman," Ana said.

Sharon also made me laugh. She sidled up to me at my husband's funeral as I sat stunned and weeping and hissed in my ear, "My great-aunt Tilly in Brooklyn was widowed when she was seventy-eight years old and remarried in a scandalous seven months." Sharon's voice was breathy and confiding. It tickled my ear, as did her red curls.

About forty-five minutes later, she cozied up to me again, "My cousin Irma was ninety-one when she was widowed, and she was remarried in five months!"

Later I asked Sharon if these stories were really true, and she still claimed they were. I could see her relatives, tiny Russian Jewish ladies, smelling of rosewater in dark New York apartments with lace doilies and potted geraniums. Like Sharon, they always managed to have a good man, until their own deaths parted them from the third or fourth.

I liked these Mexican and Jewish widows. They made me laugh. They smelled of rosewater. They smelled of change.

I had to admit, though, that friends who were bewailing their single state had less than the usual sympathy from me in the weeks after I was widowed. And people continually told me they were dreaming about me and then gave weird, New Age interpretations of the dreams. They irritated me with visions of Robert, who apparently was gallivanting all over town putting in appearances with everyone but me.

Various seekers also asked me, "Where do you think Robert went?"—as I if I were setting up as a trance medium.

"I have no idea," I would snap, losing points for spiritual correctness.

One sensible friend told me she had been dreaming about me, and instead of giving it an airy-fairy interpretation, said, "This dream means I should car-pool your daughter to school," for which I was extremely grateful. I was almost panic-stricken in my worry about Isabel.

I finally went to see Isabel's pediatrician and asked for advice. I had always loved the pediatrician, who was a contemporary woman's version of a country doctor. With her mass of graying curls and a black bag that held toys, as well as medical instruments, she had inspired confidence through bouts of scarlet fever and croupy cough. Sitting in one of the little examining rooms, I began to cry, telling the story she'd already heard about through the grapevine and obituaries.

Tears came to her eyes, too, as she reminisced about how calm Robert was and how he was the only one who could get

Isabel to hold still for the numerous throat cultures she often required for her reoccurring bouts of strep throat. She offered me a tissue.

"I bet people don't cry much in this office," I said stupidly, thinking of plump babies and energetic toddlers.

"They cry all the time," the pediatrician said, surprised.

Then it hit me; I wasn't the only person in the world who was suffering. All day long this doctor probably saw childhood leukemia and birth defects, heard tales of divorce and abuse, saw suffering in many forms, no doubt including the death of a father. I had spoken naively. I was not alone.

A friend of mine had suggested forcefully that I join a grief group at the Life Center for Attitudinal Healing, where he was on the board. I was somewhat cynical about how much a group of strangers could help me, and I already had a therapist. But I soon realized that to get through the week, I needed to have some kind of support every day. I had my therapy appointment and Isabel's; so Thursday became grief-group day.

My group was a strange assortment of folks I soon came to adore. The leader was a tiny dynamic woman, who under other circumstances might have been my friend or cousin. The members of the group at first seemed to have little in common—a widower, a man recovering from a brutal divorce, a woman with chronic health problems, and a girl who had lost a friend to suicide. The group was loose and open to anyone suffering from terrible stress or grief.

My first day I simply cried when it was my turn to talk. Through my tears, I outlined the facts, telling my story in an obsessed tone, behavior I was to see replicated by anyone who came into the group. It was as if the quest for a narrative, a story in some sensible order, was the first step to moving out of chaos.

Halloween was one ritual that came to us before we were ready. Robert had been dead only ten days before the holiday we had always enjoyed as a family was upon us. Robert had always worked with Isabel to carve a pumpkin, a feat I felt incapable of. But my friends rushed in; three different pumpkins were carved into jack-o-lanterns, and Hope took Isabel, wanly dressed in white as a little ghost, trick-or-treating with her children.

At Isabel's new school, Day of the Dead was celebrated in true Mexican style as part of the Spanish language arts program. That year the Spanish teacher was a sweet-faced guy named Ray from El Paso, just about Robert's age and a dad himself. He had taken Isabel's plight very much to heart. When it came time to build the Day of the Dead altar, Ray balked on Isabel's behalf.

"I'm going to cancel it," he told his wife.

"Stop thinking like a westerner, Ray," she shot back. Ray's wife was right; traditional cultures had had better ways of dealing with death than did our western industrial society.

Still, I went with Isabel to keep an eye on her at the school event.

An enormous altar was festooned with food, skeletons, brightly colored paper flowers, and photographs of the deceased, including someone's pet rooster and the Grateful Dead's Jerry Garcia. Isabel put Robert's picture on the altar, along with a slice of his favorite food, pepperoni pizza.

It was the middle of November, and mercifully, the weather remained dry and balmy. New Mexico was still clad in the last of its autumn colors, the gold of chamisa and the purple of asters, those two wild bushes whose blooming marked the season. I felt a particular reprieve from the weather; it lifted my spirits and kept me from the despondency that cold and rain would surely have guaranteed.

My house was still full of people, who took turns sleeping on the dirty, gray, pullout couch.

My friend and editor, Ruth, was back from a visit on the East Coast. She was a particular friend of Robert's but had missed the funeral. She appeared at the front door sobbing, bearing a container of my favorite black olives. When she stayed over, we did beauty treatments as much for the sense of consolation as for any desire for self-improvement. We put mud on our faces and henna in our hair. Ruth was beautiful enough to begin with; she had long black hair and creamy skin. Her mere physical presence was soothing.

My friend Carol was getting a divorce after a twenty-year relationship and was almost as disoriented as I. Years later she'd laugh and say that she was the only person self-engrossed enough to talk to me about *her* problems at that time. We'd lie on the unmade couch, and I'd weep quietly while Carol would talk. She may have felt guilty later, but I actually found her very consoling. Carol had an exotic almond-eyed look, and the clank of her numerous silver bracelets added a touch of gypsy. Besides, I was glad to have some company in suffering. Everyone else seemed so functional in the ordinary world.

It was the arrival of my friend Devon from Delaware, however, which signaled a new stage in my mourning: the long-distance condolence call. Devon and I had met in college, where we were both in love with the same man. When we both realized our interest was hopelessly unrequited, we became fast friends. Devon had a take-charge attitude, and even in a crisis of this magnitude, I knew she would attempt to set me on track.

Devon cooked soup and watched Isabel and me carefully for signs of imminent crackup.

She went as our cat consultant to the animal shelter in Espanola, a small town up north. The Santa Fe Shelter was out of kittens, and we needed cats—preferably two—to bring some life back to our home. There was nothing I could do about Robert's absence, but I wasn't very sentimental about my old cat's memory. If there was one thing I did not have to live without, it was kitties. Isabel immediately settled on a tiny cross-eyed kitten with an insistent voice. She named the black cat with white feet and green eyes *Felina*, which she claimed was short for Thumbe-lina. Like her mistress, Felina was chatty, bossy, and liked to zip around at high speeds.

"I found your other cat," Devon said. Walking up her arm to sit on her shoulder was a fluff ball of a black cat. He was every-thing I hadn't considered—long-haired and male—but Devon insisted. "This is a good cat," she said, "and I know good cats. Unlike your old cat," she added pointedly. She had once cat-sat my old cat Cassandra and found her obnoxious. Devon knew cats, and usually had at least a half dozen of her own.

We brought home our two new ones in a small cardboard box, which a few weeks later would not fit either of them.

I named the male *Orpheo,* for "Black Orpheus," the Brazilian movie about the Greek myth. It was a warning to myself not to look back into the land of the dead, for, of course, the poet Orpheus tries to bring his wife back to life and fails.

Orpheo adopted me immediately and followed me around like a dog. He seemed to know I was in terrible pain and would lie on my chest, staring at me encouragingly. In moments of strange fantasy, I would decide that Robert had come back in the body of a cat to comfort me, although on second thought, it seemed unlikely that my husband would have chosen to be a "fixed" cat. I had once heard someone call cats "poultices," and that is exactly what Orpheo was. He lay on my heart until it began to feel a bit better.

I could see myself through Devon's eyes as she stopped worrying so much about us. She stopped cooking and cleaning and started enjoying herself—sightseeing, shopping, visiting her Santa Fe friends. It was reassuring to me that she apparently thought I was going to make it, not crackup, kill myself, or neglect my child.

We also had an extreme moment of hilarity over a condolence letter that came to me from an old boyfriend. The condolence letters had been pouring in. They were a testament in themselves to who had loved Robert—lesbian Zen priests recounting their romances, ex-junkies swearing they were clean, old girlfriends retelling goddess-worshipping psychic experiences. It was as if people were still talking to Robert—updating him, asking for advice—even though he was dead. I put them all in a big pink hatbox.

"Save them," Devon said, as I read some of the flakiest. "They'll tell Isabel what kind of man her father was."

But this particular letter was from a very Waspy, old boyfriend of mine, who had broken my heart when I was twenty-four. For some reason we found his formal boarding-school style extremely funny. Even his taste in white stationary seemed amusing. I literally rolled on the floor laughing. It was as if I forgot for a moment that I was bereaved, concentrating on my antipathy to someone I had once adored.

Her task done, Devon felt free to go home to her job and family.

I had a deep need to be around people who had known me most of my life—the older the friend, the better. I was haunted by the sense that Robert had taken my history with him when he died—all the things he knew that no one else did.

There were two men in particular whom I wanted to talk to—Richard and Paul. I had met them at a liberal arts and sciences summer camp when we had been teenagers in the sixties. They had been friends, and I had adored them both. Paul had once put his arm around me but neglected to kiss me.

When I asked him twenty years later why he hadn't kissed me, he said simply, "I was afraid of girls."

Richard may have been afraid, too, but he had showed it less. I had been the first girl he had ever kissed, when I was fifteen and he, sixteen. We had soon progressed from there, and despite the fact that he had lived in Boston and I in New Jersey, we had established a serious relationship. We had even lived together the summer before I went to college and had been unofficially engaged, at least in our own minds. That had been before I hit my boy-crazy freshman year and realized I wasn't ready to settle down.

I had broken up with Richard in a callous manner and broken his heart. He had spent a few years hitchhiking around the country, lived on communes in California, and eventually settled down at Twin Oaks, a well-established community in Virginia. I had seen him from time to time. We had even patched up the past, with me apologizing for my behavior.

Robert and I had had a pleasant visit at Twin Oaks with Rich and his then girlfriend. Robert had enjoyed harvesting vegetables and the general ambiance, but had dismissed it as a place to live because it didn't emphasize spiritual practice.

Rich and I had continued to correspond. He eventually had left the commune, gone to library school in Boston, and gotten a straight job. In his letters he had sounded solitary, if busy with volleyball games and book groups.

I had asked my sister Rachel to call both Richard and Paul to tell them about Robert's death.

"Tell Paul to call me and Richard to write," I'd said.

Paul and I had been friends since 1967; things were more complicated with Rich. In fact, they were complicated enough that I forgot I had told Rachel to tell him not to call.

"Why hasn't he called me?" I railed.

"Because your message said not to," she reminded me, adding, "but he does sound nice. And *single*."

I had had romantic relationships almost continually my whole life. I was single for a time in my twenties, without a serious partner, but even then I had always had at least a sweetie or two, no matter how casual.

Robert and I had been together for almost fourteen years, but I found that my self-image hadn't changed too much in that time. Eventually, I would need a lover, something casual, I told myself, nice and light, a guy with his own house or someone fifty miles away in Albuquerque. I'd define a slot and keep him in it—dinner, movies, sex—but nothing more. I had a daughter to raise, a husband to grieve; I'd soon be ready for distraction, but not much else.

Of course, I felt the vague insecurity that besets most women on finding themselves single. I usually accepted my plumpness; now I felt fat. Maybe my chutzpah was wrong, my long cherished theory that I could always get a boyfriend. Maybe, as some single friends insisted, there really were no guys out there.

I still hadn't heard from Rich. Unable to stand it any longer, I called him, left a message, and he called me back. It was a Sunday night. I started talking, and I couldn't stop. Words poured out of me. I cried helplessly, endlessly. We spoke more intimately than perhaps we ever had. My usual social skin was off; I was blunt, vulnerable. He said he'd come visit some time in January, which cheered me. I needed to see a man who had known me as well as Robert had.

Robert had been dead for forty-nine days. Normally this would feel like a short amount of time, but it might have been a decade. According to Buddhist belief, his soul, which had been in a bardo space between lives, was ready to reincarnate again.

Actually, this kind of belief was held more firmly by the Tibetans than by American Zen students. However, I didn't find the concept of reincarnation very consoling. Even if Robert was born as a baby to, say, some nice Italian family in Cleveland, it didn't mean that I would ever see him again.

However, there was an important Buddhist ceremony to mark the forty-nine days, which presumably also marked the end of the formal mourning period, no matter what the exact belief was. Richard Baker-roshi, the man who had been Robert's Zen teacher, had agreed to come to the temple in Santa Fe and perform the ceremony on the fiftieth day.

The day before the ceremony, a bunch of Robert's friends were sitting around in my kitchen, drinking shots of whiskey at two in the afternoon. One of them, a serious Zen student who would later be ordained, said, "Last night at the temple, a Tibetan woman came up to me and told me not to make love that night. She said that Robert's soul might be attracted to the lovemaking and I'd end up his father."

"Did you?" I asked.

"What?"

"Make love?"

"I used a condom," said another friend of Robert's. He was on his third shot.

"You did?"

"I do not want to be Robert's father. I do not," he repeated loudly, "want to be Robert's father."

"I'd like to be Robert's mother," said Ruth, coming into the room. She drank a shot and ate a cookie.

"You had to fuck someone last night when Robert was reincarnating," I said.

"I can't believe it! I missed it! I could have been Robert's mother," said Ruth.

But the moment had passed. If Robert was going to reincarnate, it would probably be somewhere out on a lover's lane—somewhere teenagers made love recklessly in cars without condoms. We had lost him through our almost middle-aged caution. Now he would belong to someone else.

Robert himself didn't believe in reincarnation. He was essentially a rationalist, and his Buddhism contained no gods and little of other realms. Truth to tell, I didn't believe in reincarnation either. Still, I hoped the ceremony would offer consolation.

Baker-roshi had a powerful presence as a Zen teacher. He had been trained by Senryu Suzuki-roshi, one of the Japanese teachers credited with bringing Zen to America. Baker-roshi had been the abbot of San Francisco Zen Center, then departed under the shade of scandal.

Robert hadn't cared; he'd followed his teacher to New Mexico, which is why we ended up in Santa Fe. We had stayed, too, even after Baker-roshi had moved shop to a remote monastery in the southern Rockies. Robert had traveled to keep studying with Roshi, sitting weeklong sesshins in the Crestone, Colorado monastery and visiting frequently.

When Isabel was three, Robert even spent a winter there in a practice period. Isabel and I commuted two hundred miles every week to see him. The strain was enormous—winter weather, separation, the complete incompatibility of monastic and family life.

It was at the end of this practice period that Robert decided to leave Baker-roshi. There had been a great deal of tension between them towards the end, but in many ways it was a relationship I had not been privy to.

Robert would only explain obliquely. "There was a fork in the road from the first, and I finally came to it."

"Is it like ending therapy? Or getting a divorce?" I tried to put the mysterious relationship of Zen teacher and student into a more familiar context.

"No," Robert said.

"Then what?"

"I had to choose. I couldn't be his student and a father and husband as well. It was doing things to me . . . ," he said darkly.

"But I always felt you chose Baker-roshi!" I burst out. "We moved to Santa Fe for him, and I hated it . . ."

"But now you like it and won't leave!"

"Tough," I said, "It's my turn to choose. But I always felt you chose him. You waited on him hand and foot, gave him money, did things you would never do for me. You went off to Crestone in dead winter, leaving us, and I had to schlep back and forth. You used to go *grocery shopping* for that damn monastery when you wouldn't for us."

The argument could have gone on and on, but it didn't need to. Robert had left Baker-roshi. He kept his head shaved, continued to think of himself as a monk, and said he was going to find a new teacher. I was curious as to what would happen. But what

happened, after a peaceful year of ordinary life at home, was that
Robert got sick. Less than two years after that, he was dead.

Robert had seen Baker-roshi a few times when he was very ill.
The last meeting was in the oddly plastic environment of Howard
Johnson's out on the strip. Robert had been over an hour late,
which was terribly inconsiderate, I thought. Very weak, he had,
nonetheless, decided to shave his head before meeting with his old
teacher. This seemed more important to him than being on time.

"What did you talk about?" I wanted to know.

"He told me how to practice with being sick," Robert said.

I wanted to snap back, "Go to the fucking doctor and ask
more questions. Get well for God's sake. Stop practicing and get
well." But I bit back the words.

Throughout the last stages of his illness, Robert did indeed
have an eerie calm. He was cheerful, even, and mellow, despite
the physical stresses of both the disease and the mood-altering
cortisone drugs he took.

The ceremony in the small temple was a formal affair.
Robert's mother and sisters had come from the East Coast, and
the room was also crowded with at least fifty other people. We
filed in formally: I carrying the bulk of Robert's ashes, Isabel carrying a papier-mâché "healing leaf" she had once brought to her
father from a storytelling session with Rabbi Lynn Gottlieb.

I hadn't seen Baker-roshi since the winter we left the
monastery. He was in his most elaborate gold robes, very Japanese. Robert would have been pleased. Despite the Zen school's
emphasis on simplicity, he and Baker-roshi both shared a taste for
Japanese grandeur.

Baker-roshi performed the ceremony elegantly. Like most Buddhist ceremonies, it seemed to be a form of ordination, with the acceptance of a series of the familiar Bodhisattva vows. However, at the end, Baker-roshi spoke directly to Robert, his voice cracking.

"Robert," he said loudly, "we want you to know we are taking care of ourselves. Please take care of yourself, too."

That night I had scheduled a "Through the Bardo Bash" art event in Robert's memory at a local gallery, where he had performed his spoken-word gig with his bands. Poets read, a video of Robert was shown, his band played, and we hunched around a bonfire in the outer courtyard. I held a cigarette and watched the small attempt at warmth flicker at the end of my hand. I flirted with a man I had always found attractive, despite the gossip I knew about him. He even seemed to be flirting back. Something was over. In the half light of shimmering shadows, the night growing colder, it was time to let go of something and let something else begin.

But right after the ceremony in the temple, I knew I had to talk to Baker-roshi. I sat on the couch in the living room that had once been his while he changed into a simpler kimono.

We sat facing each other.

"Why did Robert leave me?" he asked.

"I don't know."

"You didn't talk about our relationship?"

"No," I shook my head.

"It was about the community at Crestone?"

I shook my head. "He always said there was a fork in the road, and he came to it." I didn't tell him the whole truth, that

Robert felt he'd been abusive. Robert might have stayed if he'd asked Robert to, if he'd shown more kindness.

"You really didn't know?"

"Did your wife understand your relationship to Suzuki-roshi?"

"Of course. I talked about it." But he looked off vaguely. Then he turned his full attention on me and said directly, "I always felt we were married to the same person, you and I, both of us married to Robert."

"Yes," I said. "I felt that way, too. Do you have any advice for me?"

"Do you know what a skandha is?" He surprised me. To the best of my limited understanding, I knew a skandha to be a technical Buddhist term, a Sanskrit word meaning an aggregate usually applied to the senses. For example, one saw through the skandha of seeing, a group of things containing, but much more than, the physical workings of the eye. There was more to it, no doubt, but I nodded yes.

"A Bodhisattva is made through the skandha of feeling. Technically. That's how it's done. Do you understand?"

I did, although I would have been hard pressed to explain it. On the one hand, I was being told to *feel my feelings*, simple advice any New Age therapist could give. On the other, Baker-roshi was implying that if I somehow lived in the aggregate of feelings, I would be transformed, and it would help those around me. It seemed too precise to be spiritual pabulum.

I looked at the tall man in a kimono, who, in effect, had been more trouble to my marriage than a host of outside women could ever have been. I could have beat out another woman, I reasoned, but I could never compete against a tall, charismatic, spiritual Zen master.

Sitting on the couch, we were both bereaved, and the relationship we had never admitted until now was finally over.

"Thank you," I told him.

My mourning period was over, and so was the seemingly endless autumn.

It was winter now in earnest, with the dark days closing in. Above New Mexico, the cold stars of the winter constellations began to wheel in their appointed turn towards the solstice. The neighborhood began to smell of the smoke of piñon and juniper, which my neighbors burned continually, starting in the earliest hours before dawn as they readied the big diesel trucks they repaired.

In some odd synergy with my state of mind, my old Toyota got four flat tires simultaneously. I went out one cold morning and found it sagging towards the ground. I had no choice but to buy four new tires. Usually this kind of task irritated me, but in my grief-stricken state of mind, I was glad to have something easy to repair. Besides, new tires were a good idea, as the first snows of winter were about to start falling.

Asia

"My feet barely touched Asian soil.
I went to bed so quickly
After a descent through a thousand
Red neon crosses
Into the Seoul airport
Above the miscellaneous quilt
Of grief . . ."

"A WIDOW IN KOREA" FROM *The Future Tense of Ash*

The weather grew cooler, leaves fell from the trees, and winter was upon us. The holidays were going to be hard. Isabel and I spent Thanksgiving weekend living in a friend's guesthouse just across town, going home every day to check on the two rambunctious kittens that never failed to lift our spirits. Still, Thanksgiving dinner was difficult without Robert. Isabel sobbed, remembering how much he liked "a heaping plate" of turkey.

It seemed impossible to get through Hanukkah, Christmas, and New Year's in our house without Robert. That is when I decided we would try to get as far away as possible and go to

Seoul, Korea, to visit Kath. My travel agent acted extremely worried. Seoul was frozen by cold, dry, Siberian winds. It was polluted. It was ugly. It sounded perfect to me. I could not remotely imagine myself somewhere pleasant like a warm island. I didn't want pina coladas and palm trees. Club Med was out of the question. Korea sounded perfect: harsh, remote, and scarred by war. It lined up with my inner frame of mind.

I bought the tickets. Isabel was very excited. She loved to travel, she loved Kath, and she liked the idea of Asia, although she wished it were China.

Our days dragged by with a sort of rhythm: work and school, a very simple dinner of noodles or stuffing, maybe chicken, broccoli, a video, then bed. She was still sleeping in bed with me, and by 8:30, I was ready for sleep, even a sleep wracked by nightmares and constant wakenings.

But the prospect of leaving the country was something to look forward to—*We're going to Korea for Christmas*—it sounded good, exotic, and enterprising.

I experienced an odd, guilty relief at only having to take care of Isabel and myself, not a sick and dying man. My role as caretaker had never been admitted between Robert and me, but it had been a grueling, at times terrifying, one. I supported us financially, cared for a small child, did all the shopping, cooking, gardening, and housekeeping.

Both Robert's and my mother had suggested I get the house cleaned regularly, which did help. But I paid all the bills, maintained the car, drove Isabel, drove Robert to his tests and procedures, and bought his diapers for him.

The last was to me the saddest task. It was something he was ashamed of, and something that was easy for me to do, but we never discussed it. Up until almost the end of his life, he always managed a bit of light cooking for himself and did his own laundry. These small tasks seemed to help him keep going.

I was leading the life of a single mother, stressful at best, and caring for an invalid, as well. The fact that we never talked about it made it harder. Robert adamantly did not want to hear any complaining from me; after all, he was the ill one and quite stoic.

The fear, of course, was much worse than any practical concerns. I cried in my car daily, afraid I couldn't keep it together financially, that we would lose the house, despite its ludicrously low mortgage and the fact that I knew rationally that, of course, my parents would help me out, if necessary. Then I would hit myself as hard as I could stand across the face and tell myself: *Shut up and make money*. I would never have treated another human being so badly, but that was how I treated myself.

Now Robert was dead, and as much as I didn't want to admit it, there was the potential for me to start taking care of myself. I tried to remember the much-touted stages of grief, but they didn't seem to apply in any linear fashion. I'd never had much denial, sad to say, because I could have used something to protect me from the shock. But it seemed as if nothing had protected me. Now I felt anger. Anger and a vague stirring of flirtatiousness. Anger, anger, anger, anger, anger, sex: Those were my stages of grief.

"Is there anything I can do for you?" That was the question Bill sent me over the grapevine. He was the most unusual of my dead husband's friends. Beat-up looking, about fifty, he'd been a professional weightlifter and still trained women. He could be hilariously funny. I'd once heard him say, "I've spent my life as the fat ladies' home companion." He was known as a run-around with the ladies but was a serious, sober alcoholic. Some of his teeth were missing; the cause he claimed was that a Great Dane had eaten his bridge when he was making love to the dog's owner, a Russian lady.

"Yes," I sent back a message to Bill. "There is something you can do for me. Show me how to lift weights."

At Mandrill's Gym, ex-felons, cops, and a smattering of suspense writers grunted and sweated. A blonde woman Bill leeringly called *the eel* coached a geezer with beautiful muscle tone.

It was dark and cold in early December, the end of a winter's afternoon. I changed out of my work clothes in the car, too disoriented to realize that, of course, there must be a changing room inside. I was still wearing my double strand of fake pearls that I liked to wear to teach in.

Bill put me first on the stationary bike, then walked me around from weight machine to weight machine. He walked with a limp, the result of a terrible car accident in which a truck had jumped the highway divide and crashed right into him. I found it easy to be around Bill because he knew what it was like to go through a hard time. And I lifted weight. It was not that different from surviving hour after hour of a crushing grief, this sensation of my arms pushing something away only to have its weight fall back on me, almost instantaneously.

"I'm a widow!" I yelled by the machine that strengthened arms. "I'm a widow!"

"That's good," Bill said.

"What's so good?"

"You didn't say it three times. If you'd said it three times, you'd really mean it."

I pondered this as Bill put me on free weights.

As I was getting ready to go, I paused by the counter to say good-bye to Bill. He and I were both distracted by the sight of one of the prettiest women I had ever seen, a cop out of uniform, a French-looking blonde in a tweed coat, a sort of roughness burnishing her.

"Billy . . ." She wanted his attention.

"Give me a minute," he said, indicating me. "I want to kiss this woman good-bye."

"Well," said the blonde, staring at me, "I can see why." Her voice was slow, erotic, full of the nuance of a pass.

I fled. I was a widow, I was a widow, but apparently I was now also a single woman in a gym full of possibilities. The cobalt-blue air of winter's evening cooled my hot cheeks. I was out the door of Mandrill's, but not until I heard Bill shout after me, "Next time, can the pearls."

Classes ended. It was winter in earnest, and just ten days before we were supposed to go to Korea Isabel came down with a severe, croupy cough. We were up each night, steaming in the shower, spooning cough medicine.

The nurse practitioner at our pediatrician's office offered, "If this is your dream vacation, just go. I think she'll be well enough."

I looked at him. Korea in dead winter was hardly anyone's idea of a dream vacation, but I took his advice.

Isabel and I flew to L.A. and waited out the long stopover before we boarded our flight across the Pacific. After Santa Fe, even LAX seemed exotic. We ate delicious pizza, changed some of our money, and napped on our coats. I had bought Isabel a tiny, traveling game set, and we played endless hours of snakes and ladders, checkers, chess.

One side effect of being grief-stricken was that I was so enervated that I was seldom bored. Normally I was an impatient person, sometimes to the point of New-York-style rudeness. Normally, the idea of taking a lively six-year-old child with croup halfway around the world would have terrified me. But it felt as if the worst had already happened. We had hit bottom. Little fazed me. Months later, my old personality returned, and I would look back with a kind of nostalgia at my mental calm.

The flight lasted over twelve hours. We slept, woke to stewardesses in Korean national costume, handing us hot steaming cloths, ate, slept, drank tiny glasses of fruit juice. The stewardesses seemed to change outfits about six times, in a kind of entertaining pantomime.

Isabel's cough had indeed eased up, and she was a good traveler.

My favorite aspect of the flight was a video screen, which lit up periodically showing a map of the world with our own plane on it, how many miles traveled and for how long, to the second. It recorded the speed of the headwinds and showed our tiny plane cross Alaska, the International Date Line, and the vast blue ocean, and then head towards Asia. Artificial as it was, it gave me a sense of location, as if inner experience could be expressed outwardly.

We finally landed and cleared customs easily, despite my fear that all the croup medication might look like contraband. Many of our fellow travelers were servicemen or their families.

Kath was standing at the barrier and waving. She was wearing Robert's favorite black-and-brown wool vest that I had given her after the funeral.

Kath took us home in a black taxicab, explaining the gray taxis were cheaper; the black were fancier. Indeed, the driver was dressed like the doorman of a fine hotel. He, like practically every Korean we met, commented on Isabel's beautiful pink cheeks.

Kath had traveled many times in China, and she had a bad habit of mixing up her languages. As an English teacher, she did not have much need for Korean, and despite her uncanny ability to pick up some of any language, she often reverted to speaking Mandarin by mistake, particularly to taxi drivers. However, we soon learned how to give the proper address: *Gook Dong Apartu*—Far East Apartments.

The Gook Dong Apartu was in a modest, ugly complex in a neighborhood that looked as if Stalin had redone New York's Chinatown. Most of the building had been constructed after the war and was cheap and standardized. As we walked up the three flights to Kath's apartment, we caught an overwhelming smell—fermenting kim chee. I was one of the few Americans I knew who actually loved the Korean national delicacy of hot pickled cabbage, and I was looking forward to the varieties in Seoul. But in the Far East Apartments, every family had their own vat fermenting on a balcony, and the smell was nasty, even for an aficionado.

Kath's apartment also smelled faintly of the drains that periodically backed up. Yet it was an oddly appealing and cozy place—two bedrooms, tiny living room, and tinier kitchen.

Kath's roommate was gone for the holidays, and Isabel and I had her room, perfectly tidy, with two, thin Korean-style futons on the linoleum, a floor made delightful by the radiant heat, which pulsed reliably from it.

There was even a stack of presents for Isabel, a Christmas tree, and the decoration that Kath favored everywhere she lived and at any season—strings of colored Christmas lights.

It was also the last night of Hanukkah. I whipped out a little menorah and nine wax candles and lit them. Kath had to laugh. She hated Jewish holidays, and I was always trying to drag her off to celebrate this or that. Now Hanukkah had come to Seoul, Korea.

But if I thought I could escape Christmas by going to Asia, I was wrong. Even flying into the airport, I had noticed the city lit up below us, many of the tall buildings adorned with red neon crucifixes. Korea had also adopted the holiday as much for its western, secular customs as for its religious ones, and everything was covered with decorations. As a Jew, I had always felt alienated from the day and the season.

But in the States, I did enjoy certain rituals at the homes of friends, who had some spiritual sense of the holiday. Often Robert and I had gone to see the Mattachine dance at the pueblo of San Juan. His last Christmas Eve, he had gone with a friend, the drummer in his band who was from the pueblo, to see the Indian dance, which derived from medieval Spanish court dancing, by firelight. It had been very cold, and he'd been weak, but thrilled to do it. I remember I had worried about his ability to drive the long stretch of highway.

Still, if I couldn't escape Christmas, I had escaped the familiar. We slept a jet-lagged sleep, waking frequently. Isabel was amazed at how the great city itself didn't sleep; there was the noise of sirens and traffic all night. I'd been born in Manhattan, and so it was oddly familiar, comforting even, to feel the great anonymous buzz of urban life.

On Christmas Day, we went off to the Westin, one of the fanciest hotels in Seoul, to see Kath's current boyfriend play the saxophone. He was a sweet-faced, black guy from Brooklyn, who made part of his living from gigs like this, in residence for a few months with a band somewhere in Asia where taste ran to the retro in music. Kath had abbreviated his name and called him *the B-dude*. He wore a hat given to him by a Nigerian diplomat and a beautiful New-York-style coat of expensive black wool. He was also a first-rate musician, although worn down by the necessity of playing classic lounge jazz night after night when he had a Master's in musicology and an interest in the contemporary.

Robert would have liked the B-dude and been interested in his music. Robert would have paid attention, asked questions, bought tapes or cassettes the B-dude recommended. After Robert died, about fifty people tried to return things to me that Robert had lent them—books, magazines, cassettes, and Xeroxes. He had even found a Petula Clark record for Ruth and lent it to her.

Of course, I told all just to keep whatever Robert had given them. He liked nothing more than matching a person to the right literature or music.

I sighed and said to Kath, "If Robert were alive at home, I'd have to grill the B-dude to find out what music he liked, who he studied with."

"Robert would have cared," she said. "More than we do."

Kath had always asked Robert for romantic advice. Now she had a boyfriend Robert would never meet. The world was going along as it always had, relentlessly. Never had the division between life and death seemed so great.

Even without Robert to report to, I admired the B-dude's ability to bring the saxophone to life, to soar and glide, even when playing to a buffet-eating hotel audience of wealthy Americans and Asians.

And what a buffet! It was one of the best I had ever seen or eaten. Food had been a problem for me. I couldn't taste it, didn't want it, forgot all about it. I lost a few pounds, but mostly I just got dizzy periodically and felt as if I were about to black out. That buffet may have been the first thing that looked good to me in two-and-a-half months, and it was lavish with delicacies. It had a complete American brunch with eggs cooked to order and bacon, ham, and sausage. There was a huge Chinese buffet of hot chafing dishes. In between were sushi rolls and the omnipresent kim chee.

We later discovered that the usual cheap Korean sushi rolls sold in grocery stores were made with spam. Isabel loved them and raves about them to this day, but, of course, Kath and I were revolted.

We ate, listened to the band play, and almost fell asleep on the comfortable sofas. Soon it was dark again outside. We had made it through the great hurdle of Christmas, and in a pleasant, if strange enough fashion.

After that, our visit to Korea fell into a lulling, eccentric rhythm. Kath was fighting a bad cold, and even when well, had an aversion to the usual tourist sights of temples and museums. Instead, we walked down a long flight of cement steps out of Gook Dong Apartu, crossed a broad avenue under a light sprinkling of snow, and went down a short flight of stone steps, made slippery by moisture, to the women's baths.

The baths, both traditional and modern in feel, were another world. They reminded me of the Japanese baths I'd loved in San Francisco, but were more intense.

We changed in a modern locker room, and naked, entered the steamy tiled room of the baths. The temperatures of the waters were extreme—boiling hot and freezing cold—but the heat was very relaxing once you could tolerate it. Every woman and child, about thirty people, stared boldly at us—the naked white ladies and child.

Isabel's cheeks were bright pink in the steam, and complete strangers would come up to her and rub them to see if the pink would come off.

Kath and I, from Mediterranean stock, had larger breasts than the Korean ladies, who checked them out.

We, in turn, checked out the way they wrapped their heads in red-and-pink scarves and unabashedly shaved their legs in public.

Most fascinating were the massages going on in full view of the bathers. The clients lay down naked on tables while the masseuses climbed on top and pummeled them in the most rapid-fire shiatsu-like massage I had ever seen. The masseuses were dressed, very oddly, we thought, in sets of black bras and panties. We could never figure out why they worked in their underwear instead of in bathing suits, as if somehow the underwear gave a sense of required modesty.

The baths provided an almost daily respite from the cold. The soaking seemed to help Isabel and me emotionally, as well.

Despite the excitement of travel, and the comfort of seeing Kath, we were still in very bad shape. I had attacks of feeling dizzy on the street and was much too timid to explore on my own.

Kath told me later she finally realized how messed up I was when I refused to take a taxi anywhere alone—I, a New Yorker, who liked nothing better than taxis, and who in general was more at home in a strange city than in the woods.

The mixture of agoraphobia and grief had one nice side effect. Isabel and I explored every inch of the area of the Gook Dong, and in this way came to know and love a small corner of an exotic world. There is something to be said for intense observation of something obscure, and that was exactly what our visit to Korea entailed.

Right out the door was a small strip of shops, which we perused intently. There was the tiny narrow stationery store, where we bought stickers, the Japanese Hello Kitty line of stationery, and paper dolls.

There were wonderful stationery stores all over the city, many in the underground malls that ran along the subway stations, and I came home with a bag full of notebooks and pencil cases. I particularly liked the odd way English was used to decorate items—my silver-colored pencil case said *Generation X: 1975* on it for no apparent reason. (Of course, I knew Western design was also to blame; I had socks and earrings at home emblazoned with Chinese characters, whose meanings were completely unknown to me.) We visited the stationery store in the neighborhood almost daily to buy Isabel a little something.

Then there was the bakery. Like most Korean bakeries, it was full of things that looked good, but were not quite to our taste. Much of it was sponge cake, which tasted of cardboard. Baked dessert is not a natural in that part of the world, and Kath instructed us, "When it comes to the pastries of Asia, you just have to keep trying until you find what you like." With this advice in hand, we tried several things a day. Isabel finally settled on white French rolls, I on a pastry stuffed with bean curd.

There was a small dark grocery store, where men sat around a kerosene heater, playing some kind of gambling game with tiles. The window featured a display of holiday baskets: tangerines with a centerpiece of cans of spam.

There was also a video store with English language videos for rent. Isabel settled on Disney's *The Lion King* and began to watch it over and over. At first Kath and I were concerned, although it did give us an adult hour in which to talk. Then we realized why she was watching it. The hero's father is killed, and he thinks it is his fault. Bereavement and guilt with eventual redemption;

that was the plot of the movie. The story had become some kind of comfy blanket for Isabel, and we let her watch.

Behind the apartment building was another market, two-storied and more exciting. In my generally reduced state, a trip with Isabel across the field and into the market was high adventure.

Once inside, we were greeted by a bustling food market with live fish in tanks and small stalls serving take-out and stir-fry.

A lady stopped us and politely handed Isabel a free tangerine. Then the lady pushed a tiny boy from behind the counter so he could have a look at the exotic, red-cheeked American child.

In this obscure neighborhood, Isabel was a perhaps never-before-seen novelty. Indeed, most Koreans were used to servicemen, and no one else, as representatives of America. And as Kath pointed out, most Americans stuck to the bases or the tourist attractions and would never enter the Gook Dong. But I liked it and was content to carry home large baggies full of different kinds of kim chee to try.

One afternoon we all went to have our hair cut at Marie's Hair Art across from the bakery. Inside, it was like the 60's, a tiny shop full of brightly colored equipment and photos of old-fashioned styles pulled from magazines and pasted to the mirrors.

Marie cut all of our hair carefully. Kath and Isabel got trims, but I had my hair cut much shorter than Robert had liked it.

Marie wanted to know about the United States. "How much does a haircut cost in Los Angeles?"

"An inexpensive one in a salon, about thirty dollars. But it could probably go up to a hundred."

Marie shook her head in wonder. "I want to move to Los Angeles," she said, blowing my hair dry.

Our favorite place for lunch was a Japanese-style restaurant run by Koreans near the baths. Isabel ate heaping baskets of udon noodles. She was only six years old, but those fat white noodles imprinted on her as the perfect food. She talked about them frequently upon our return and often suggested we go back to Korea to have more. It wasn't until three years later that she found them again in San Francisco's Japan town. But they did not come in a two-layered basket as in Korea, where, when you finished the first layer, you lifted up the cover and found another layer steaming beneath.

Despite the good food, Kath pointed out that we could never seem to get through a meal without sobbing. And, she griped, we couldn't seem to coordinate our despair.

"First, you'll be fine and Isabel will be sobbing about Robert, then she'll cheer up, and you'll go off."

We may not have had a peaceful moment to eat without hysterics, but Kath was also implicated. Although not as bad as Isabel and me, she would cry without warning. One time a discussion of dentists set her off. "Robert loved the dentist," she sobbed. "And he took such good care of his teeth." Robert had taken good care of his teeth, and he did like the dentist, who often didn't charge him because he was a monk. Soon we were all crying over our noodles.

The only major expedition that Kath actually planned for us was to the fabled Lotte (pronounced "Latte," as in caffé latte) World. This was an enormous underground mall that ran many city blocks and was so huge the life-sized replica of the Trevi Fountain—a surprising sight in any case—was a minor landmark in its vastness.

Lotte World also housed an amusement park in acreage that would have been worthy of Disneyland. Completely enclosed, its artificial light gave it a dream-like quality, enhanced by the fake hot air balloons, which circled its distant ceiling.

Accompanying us to Lotte World was an English student of Kath's, a young man who hoped to study engineering in the United States. He was a nice young guy, and Isabel attached to him immediately, as she did to any man who showed an avuncular interest in her after Robert's death.

We arrived early in the painted, artificial paradise before the crowds. Kath did point out the numerous wedding couples, who were having their official portraits taken there, though, the brides all in formal, western-style white dresses.

Isabel was extremely excited by the rides. I vetoed an enormous pirate ship that swung recklessly from side to side, full of screaming riders. (She finally made it on such a ride at the New Mexico State Fair when she was almost ten and admitted that it was nauseating.) We settled on a sequence of fairly scary rides, anyway.

We took boats through a haunted house with a Sinbad theme with the usual skeletons popping out at us. We also took boats down fast chutes that sprayed us with water. Afraid of heights, I really hated this kind of thing, but agreed to go. My terror was a new feeling, the first time I had felt afraid of anything external since Robert's death. Kath got soaked, which made her cold worse.

On the way home, we stopped in a pharmacy, where, much to my surprise, the pharmacist prescribed various antibiotics and cough medicines for her. No doctor's prescription was needed here. Kath, not completely satisfied with her doses, called her dad, a doctor in Albuquerque, to get his input on her imminent bronchitis. The world seemed both large and small at that moment.

With Kath somewhat out of commission with her cold and Isabel content to watch *The Lion King* repeatedly, I was often alone with my own thoughts and feelings.

I was finally able to read again. After Robert died, reading became impossible. I did not have the concentration to follow the simplest thing. My brain no longer seemed to work. In the cocoon of Kath's warm-floored apartment, I was able to slog through a Victorian murder mystery. It was as difficult for me to read that paperback as it might have been to read scientific theory or French philosophy. Reading did not induce the trance it usually did; I could not lose myself in a book. But things soon got easier.

Kath's roommate had worked in the Sudan, and a book written by a Sudanese woman was lying by the futon. It was a horrifying account of female circumcision, forced marriage, and escape. It was the first book that compelled me since Robert died, and I read every word.

That was the start of a course of reading about extreme states, the worse the better. I even went through a phase of reading every word to come out of the doomed Everest expedition; even if I had no interest in mountain climbing, I was interested in death. I read accounts of ships that went down in storms and of women who went off to Antarctica. I obviously felt I had suffered something extreme myself and was trying to understand it through these adventures.

Several years after Robert's death, I found myself browsing in a chain bookstore, ostensibly looking for a book on Scott's doomed South Pole expedition, which combined a lot of my favorite themes—cold, isolation, extremis, death.

"What are you looking for?" the clerk asked helpfully.

"Accounts of extreme states," I blurted out to the puzzled young man.

"I don't think we have a section on that," was all he could say to an obviously eccentric patron.

Of course, I also wanted to read about widows. Back home, I checked out every book I could find on the topic in the public library, but found little that helped me. The average book was kindly, but much too generic. It usually advised me on things my husband had presumably done, such as change the oil and manage the money. Such books seemed more geared to widows of my mother's generation. The few accounts by women my age seemed more narratives of desolation than recovery.

I excitedly found one book by a woman who was preparing to swim the English Channel when she was suddenly widowed. Naively, I just assumed she'd go ahead and swim anyway. I was looking forward to her triumph when the book devolved into a mini-breakdown in her New York apartment instead. I was bitterly disappointed. I wanted her to swim.

In Dr. Joyce Brother's book on widowhood, she admitted that she couldn't masturbate and left her sexual life at that.

Sex, however, was higher on my list of concerns than automobile maintenance.

In Korea, I made a mental list of everyone I knew who might qualify as a potential lover. My list was undiscriminating; it included people who lived thousands of miles away, the perhaps about-to-be divorced, those with bad reputations, and some I hadn't met.

Sharon had told me in a strict voice, "You are not ready to date. But when you are—and I will tell you when I think you are—I will fix you up with this nice guy I know in Albuquerque who has a boat."

Luckily I was with Kath, who found my list idea more amusing than shocking.

"But first," I told her, "I have to see what happens when Richard visits. Then I'll start on the list."

Indeed, my other friends were much less amused by my forthrightness. They'd known me for a dozen years as a conventional wife and mom. My really old friends, who'd known me during much wilder times, just rolled their eyes and mentioned that safe sex had come into fashion.

I had no intention of remaining alone. Unstated by those around me was the assumption that I should somehow remain faithful to Robert. But I realized that both by the laws of Judaism and those of the State of New Mexico, I was a free agent. I decided what I wanted: a lover or two, nice guys, nothing heavy, people I could go to the movies with, preferably men with their own houses and lives, who would stay out of my hair.

Isabel, I resolved, would know nothing of these casual dates.

But my thoughts did dwell on Richard. We had a long and complex history. He had been my first lover, and I, his. His skinny body, his soft skin, his narrow handsome face, his brown eyes, and his occasionally perplexed squint—all were imprinted on me. We had spent hours, days, exploring each other. It was a sensual, gratifying relationship. Only after I was an adult did I realize how lucky I was not to have lost my virginity, like so many others, at a party, in the back of a car, or on a casual date.

We got on equally well out of bed. We shared museums, walks, city neighborhoods, books, music, the ocean. Shy at first, he was a chatty person who could express his thoughts and feelings. We got on with each other's families, each other's friends.

The only thing that had been allegedly missing from our intimate relationship was a declaration of love. Richard refused to say he loved me. Yes, he wanted to be with me, but as a young cynic he scorned the notion of romantic love.

When my first college boyfriend started in declaring helplessly that he loved me—I was hooked. Although in many ways he and I were much less compatible than I had been with Rich, this seemed to be the missing ingredient.

What Richard and I had had was puppy love, I decided; it had lacked depth, emotional passion.

But now I was weirdly fixated on him. I decided that he would be the perfect first post-widowhood lover for me. After all, he'd known me when I was a sexually incompetent, hysterical, weepy teenager. I wasn't so different now. I didn't take his needs or feelings into consideration in these fantasies. After all, I really did not have a clear idea of what kind of man he had become. Still, I was a woman who had always liked a plan.

Before we left Korea, Kath did decide on one afternoon of tourist delights. We went to the old part of town, with traditional teahouses and architecture, with the B-dude.

But first, he had to replace the reeds in his saxophone's mouthpiece, and off we went to yet another indoor arcade that consisted only of about two dozen music shops. One shop sold only violins; one sold only electric pianos. The B-dude went to the saxophone store, where he was well-known, and replaced the part.

The old section of Seoul was cluttered with ancient-looking, wooden buildings with thatched roofs. I left the others in a teahouse, playing checkers with Isabel, and went off by myself for a precious half hour alone. I admired stores selling a variety of paint brushes, ranging in size from a mascara brush to an artist's calligraphy one. In a jewelry store I bought three pendants: a jade Kwan-yin for Hope, an amber one for Sharon, and a branched piece of hot-pink coral for Ruth. Despite the dusty smell and dim light, the shopkeeper was glad to accept my plastic credit card and verify it by phone.

Our last day in Seoul was so cold that we could only manage a small expedition underground. A few subway stops took us to the underground flower market, which ran for twisty block after block.

Real roses mingled with all kinds of fake finery. Trees made of blue, glittery wire and climbing vines of gold plastic seemed like something out of a stage set for a fairy tale.

In the adjacent costume-jewelry arcade, booth after booth sold rhinestone pins and shining objects of adornment. This was Korea shortly before the Asian market crashed, still booming.

Isabel bought herself a headband on top of which perched a golden butterfly whose wings fluttered with the slightest movement.

That afternoon, Isabel and I took one last trip down the cement stairs out of the Gook Dong and on to the avenue. We bought a large, ceramic pig bank that she had admired, carried it home, and promptly dropped it, breaking it on the floor of the apartment. Back we went for another one, a Korean piggy bank painted in bright pink and good-luck red.

Our mission safely accomplished, we stopped for an ice cream cone. In the familiar ambiance of Baskin Robbins, we each ordered a scoop—chocolate for her, rainbow sherbet for me. We sat at a little table and played a game of snakes and ladders, that ancient board game from India, which apparently represents the world of karma, of cause and effect, where anything can happen. At the shake of a dice, a player can climb a ladder, or with a reverse of fortune, fall backwards through a snake's mouth. It is often played in the United States as chutes and ladders, but our tiny traveling set had the traditional serpents lounging across the board. We shook the dice, and by mutual agreement, did not play to win, but continued playing until both she and I had safely completed the round.

Boyfriend

"Things change—you throw a stone in the pond
Freeze frame on a ripple
Call that ripple "my life"—my marriage, my house,
*   my child*
From a star in the Andromeda galaxy
That ripple barely exists
Pond too small to see
Let alone the stone in your palm."

"A New Autobiography" from *The Widow's Coat*

"It takes a hundred days to come off heroin," a been-there-done-
that friend told me. "And so I expect you will feel better in about
three months."

Robert had been dead more like a mere two-and-a-half
months, but I was starting to feel, if not exactly better, more as if
I could function. Isabel and I came home jet-lagged from Korea
and slept close to twenty hours. Then I told her, as we had
agreed, it was time for her to sleep in her own bed. This gave me
an instant reprieve; I could stay up a little later than 8:30 P.M.,

even watch a bit of a video or read a magazine. Time alone was refreshing; I could even enjoy it.

School began for Isabel; I still had a few weeks of break.

I had spent a fair amount of money going to Korea, but I expected to make it up because I was in the process of suing Social Security for all the disability money that was owed Robert, who had been denied it twice. My attorney correctly assumed that we would win, in part because of the sad irony that Robert was dead. So I was glad to have additional time before I returned to work.

Richard was coming to visit. This event loomed obsessively in my mind. "Put him up at the El Rey Motel," one worried friend advised.

Other friends kept suggesting I travel more, or re-stucco the house, or get a full-time job. But these things didn't seem to function as an outlet for my feelings. And surely, I reasoned, on this planet of so many billions, there was someone who might cheer me up a little.

So I arranged a sleepover for Isabel and set out to meet Richard's plane at the Albuquerque airport. For some unsubstantiated reason, I was convinced I would go to bed with him. It had been fourteen years since I had slept with any man other than my husband, and yet the fantasy persisted. Maybe it was easier to fantasize about an old boyfriend than a scary new one.

"Get condoms and nightgowns," a chic friend had instructed me for dating in middle age.

I actually went to Dillard's and bought two new nightgowns. One was a demure, but skimpy, white cotton, the other a slinky paisley number with lace. This act alone should have shown me how serious I was. I had literally never bought myself two night-gowns. Robert was uninterested in such things, and I tended to sleep in funky, old, comfortable ensembles. But now I had night-gowns.

If my more conservative friends wanted Richard ensconced at the El Rey, my single, dating friends had lots of advice about condoms, recommending different brands.

The most direct advice came from one friend, who bluntly said, "If you can find a middle-aged guy who can make love wear-ing a condom, keep him."

Apparently male sexual dysfunction was as much of a con-cern as safe sex. It had been a long time since I was single.

Late that afternoon, before I headed out, I had an unpleas-ant errand to run. My lawyer wanted me to pick up all of Robert's medical records from St. Vincent's Hospital in Santa Fe to pre-pare for our hearing with Social Security.

Robert had been hospitalized briefly at St. Vincent's when he collapsed a few days before his surgery was scheduled. Then he had been moved to Presbyterian Hospital in Albuquerque, where he had died. I was morbidly glad that he hadn't died in St. Vincent's, because I passed it almost every day. I also man-aged to hold on to some positive associations with the place, because Isabel had been born there. Still, it was going to be a hard job to walk into any hospital, particularly one where Robert had been.

Pulling into the parking lot, I began to pray, "Just let me get through this, give me some support, help me get through this."

My prayer was answered, although in an unexpected way. There, coming out of a car parked in a handicapped space was Bill, the weightlifter, on his lame leg. We chatted for a moment, and then he looked at me suggestively and kissed me. I started giggling like a fourteen-year-old. I knew by now I wasn't really interested; still, an encounter with Bill always cheered me up. If I was worried that Richard would find me hopelessly plump and middle-aged, not to mention morose, it was good to know I wasn't completely unattractive. I was also so distracted that I breezed in and out with the records, without breaking into tears or having an anxiety attack.

I had supper with Sharon at a nice restaurant near the airport. She loved the Kwan-yin pendant I'd brought her back from Korea. She also took in my apparent slightly improved mental state and said she was ready to fix me up with the guy with the boat.

Armed with the promise, like a talisman, of a guy with a boat, I felt prepared to meet Richard's plane. He had been called Frodo, Rico, Ricardo, Rich, and Rocky after the flying squirrel. I settled on the most formal, Richard, as if to maintain a little distance between us.

It was quite late at night when his plane arrived. He got off toting several bags, plopped them down, asked me to watch them, and went to the men's room.

I was immediately irritated. There was nothing romantic about this reunion, and his lugging of bags and newspapers reminded me he had been that way in our youth, always walking quickly, carrying something unwieldy, ignoring me.

Still, even in the harsh fluorescent light, he looked as cute as ever. He was skinny and handsome with a slightly sheepish expression. The only thing that was different was that his hair was gray at the temples instead of pure black.

I drove us back up La Bajada Hill along the dark highway, rapidly firing questions at Richard.

"Tell me about B., the woman who broke your heart in graduate school. Why did she leave you?"

"It's a little early in the visit to get into that."

"Well then, why are you still single? Why hasn't some cute Boston woman grabbed you? I know at least five women I could fix you up with!"

He seemed startled, even a little offended. "I haven't been with a woman in four years."

"How weird," I continued tactlessly. "That's not how I remember you at all."

"Look," he said, "I've had quality, but not quantity, in my relationships. You broke up with me; then things with T. ended after seven years. After I left the commune, P. broke up with me, which was devastating."

"Then B?"

"Then B."

"You should keep away from women with femmy names, names that end in double 'e'. Like P., B . . ."

"Not T."

"No. She always seemed right for you."

"But it ended."

"So?"

"So I decided I needed to figure out what I wanted. I want a serious committed relationship, with or without formal marriage; I want to spend my life with someone."

"Should she be young? Old? Want children or not? Have them?" Of course, I was fishing for information.

"Not too young, someone close to my age. Children . . . either way. But it has to be serious. I'd have to go out with someone for at least six months before going to bed."

"Six months!" I almost drove off the road. "I don't think of you that way at all! Six months! That is completely dumb."

"It's kind of rude to call a person's decision dumb," he said.

"I'm sorry. But it just doesn't sound like you."

"It is me."

"But you love sex!"

"I've been hurt," he said, "too many times. I'm not going to keep making the same mistake over and over."

"You could die at any moment, be hit by a truck. You can't live for the future."

"I want to get married," he said.

We sped along in silence. This guy is not for me, I thought. Six months! I was in a rush. He, in my opinion, was retreating from life. Too bad. I looked up and saw a huge shooting star off to the east. How romantic. What a waste.

"What about you?" he asked.

"Oh, I'm really messed up from Robert's death. Still, I'm ready to date," I said fliply. "This guy has already kissed me, and my friend Sharon is getting ready to fix me up with some guy with a boat."

"Sounds like your dance card is full," Richard said, without the slightest indication that he wanted to be on it.

Still, at my house I gave it one more try. I put on the white nightgown, the chaste of the two new ones, and invited Richard to sit on my bed and talk. "You could sleep with me *platonically*," I suggested, "or I can put you up in the guest room."

"The guest room is fine," he said, much to my disappointment. After all, I hadn't shared a bed with a man, even platonically, since Robert had fallen ill. But apparently, this was not to be.

The next day was a pleasant, if non-flirtatious, one. After picking up Isabel from Hope's and taking her to school, I showed Richard the town. We looked at churches and galleries, drove up to the ski basin, ate lunch at one of my favorite bistros. It was good to be with an old friend, to catch up, to talk and talk. I cried convulsively every few hours, speaking about Robert. Richard listened with quiet compassion. He was a real friend. But it was no more than that.

That evening, Richard went out to the movies with a friend of his, who, by coincidence, was visiting Santa Fe. I was exhausted and asleep by eight o'clock. I had given up on my romantic fantasies. I figured he really wasn't interested in me. I was too fat, and I cried too much, often blowing my nose. Besides, it would take him at least six months to figure out if he was interested in me, and all we had was three days.

The next day I had planned a trip to the hot springs at Ojo Caliente, about an hour north of Santa Fe and one of my favorite places on earth. It had a series of pools and tubs at different temperatures, full of hot water in which were dissolved different kinds of therapeutic minerals. It felt far away and funky.

A broad veranda framed the old hotel, and desert hills came down to a small river. I could see immediately that Richard was entranced. He turned his attention to Isabel, who was splashing in the warm swimming pool. She latched on to him, soon creating a game in which he dove beneath a tent barrier, dividing a warm area from a cooler one, with her on his back.

"Two-headed dragon! Two-headed dragon!" she cried, christening the game.

Looking at them, they might have been father and daughter; they looked so alike. Indeed, Robert and Richard were of a type: short, dark-haired, brown-eyed.

I felt increasingly melancholy. But the water was wonderfully soothing, and we had a nice lunch in the little cafe and a walk through cottonwood bosque along the river to the site of an old corral.

It was so warm that January afternoon that Richard took off his shirt as we strolled. He carried Isabel back to the car on his shoulders.

Late that afternoon, I dropped Isabel off at Talaya's house for a sleep over. When I had set it up, I had no doubt anticipated some romance; now I was just glad for the break.

Back home, I found myself sitting on the couch with Richard, weeping again. Perhaps it was partially the stress of the day, of wanting some kind of happiness again, that set me off. I couldn't seem to stop sobbing.

Richard suddenly said, "Can I hug you?"

I looked up, surprised, and scooted towards him.

We put our arms around each other, and I abruptly felt consoled and at peace. We fell together and lay like that for a long time. There was something about his body I had never noticed before; it seemed to hum in some mysterious manner. It was like standing next to a refrigerator compressor or beneath high-tension wires. Had he always had this effect on me, or was it just the magic of the moment? We started kissing, biting each other's lips, kisses that led nowhere as if we were fourteen years old again and bound by the mysterious laws of adolescent chastity.

It was time for dinner. I was ready to cancel and lie on the couch forever, but Richard always believed in eating a solid meal, in good times and bad. We went out to dinner to the Old Mexico Grill. The restaurant was a favorite of mine. Even though it was essentially in a strip mall, it had a nice ambiance of folk art and the good smell of grilling on charcoal.

My lips felt chapped as we shared a salad, hot sauce, chicken. A flush permeated us, but no one in the restaurant seemed to notice.

"Have you ever wondered," Richard asked, "when you look around a restaurant, what is really going on with people?"

"Their secrets—hates, loves, fears?"

"Yes."

"Like no one looking at us could tell what was going on," I said, not that I knew what was going on.

Richard chewed seriously and nodded.

"You look like you're afraid of me," I said.

"I am afraid of you."

"Why?"

"Because you are a conduit for strong emotion."

"I'm a human being," I said.

"I'm afraid of myself, too," he said.

I moved closer to him in the booth. Heat seemed to radiate from him, and he smelled of salsa.

At home, we spent more hours on the couch, touching, cuddling, but not going over some invisible line that seemed to exist only in Richard's mind.

We walked in some ancient Indian ruins the next day. Sun and stone failed to distract me. Richard touched my back briefly with two fingers of one hand, and it burned through my shirt.

"I'll come visit you in Boston," I said, "but only if you'll have sex with me."

"O.K.," he said.

"We'll come in March, on spring break."

"In March? The weather is horrible then!"

He still didn't get it. "I'm coming to see you," I said. "I'm not coming for the weather!"

He looked dubious.

"You have to surrender to me," I said. I didn't know where these words were coming from.

"How will you know if I have?"

"I'll know." I said. "We have unfinished business," I added, "and one way or another, I am going to finish it."

That Sunday evening, we might have been any family in a normal domestic routine. Richard played chess and checkers with Isabel on her little traveling board; we ordered a pizza. I read her a good-night story and tucked her in to bed. Now, chaperoned by my impulse not to confuse my daughter, Richard had to head to the guest room.

"I guess I blew my chance," he said. He was getting on a plane the next morning. This was our last night.

"Not completely. You can't sleep with me all night because of Isabel, but come to bed with me now. But I have to warn you; if she cries or knocks, I'll get up, no matter what we're doing. Just be quiet," I said and led him into my bedroom. I locked the door behind us.

We lay down naked. When we started to make love, it hurt, literally hurt as if death or marriage were a hymen.

Soon I lost control of my breath. I was hyperventilating, in need of carbon dioxide, overdosing on oxygen. I heard my husband Robert breathing in his coma. He was wrapped in warm plastic sheeting, although his body was blue. At this high altitude, he was long brain dead, and he had been a man with an amusing brain. I heard his breath, too regular, too shallow, controlled from the outside, the breath of a machine, laboring towards something—extinction. I was having a flashback, as vivid as reality.

Then I was able to control it, to come back to the present.

"Are you O.K.?" I asked Rich, concerned that he also was flipping out in some way.

"O.K. is not exactly the word I would use." He laughed, blissing out.

It seemed strange after that to make him sleep in the guest room, but I did. I wanted to protect Isabel from her mother's peccadilloes.

The next morning we drove Rich to the shuttle bus to the airport. He and I embraced madly, kissing on the sidewalk.

"I think you should marry him," Isabel announced from the back seat as we drove home.

"Honey, you don't just marry people."

"You kissed him," she pointed out. "And he's nice."

A few days passed, and I did not hear from Rich. Somehow, I knew to just call him. I left a message on his answering machine, thanking him for his visit, and saying, "You opened my heart." Although I was the widow, he was the one who had been single all those years. I knew he needed reassurance.

He called back quickly, admitting, "I was fine—happy, even—for a day or two. Then I had a terrible anxiety attack on the trolley coming home from work. I kept thinking: What have I done?"

"We'll come visit in March," I said.

"I figured I shouldn't pressure you. Maybe this was nothing, just a wonderful experience with an old friend. I figure I should leave you alone until you recover. Maybe next fall . . ."

"I wouldn't do that if I were you."

"Why not?"

"Because I'm apt to just take up with someone else. It could take me years to recover, but I won't wait around for that. If you want me, better go for it."

"Well, I want a serious long-term relationship—a commitment."

"Sure."

"Like getting married."

"Sure."

"I gather you didn't hear what I said to you in bed after we made love."

"No. What?" Whatever it was, he must have murmured it as if to himself.

"I love you."

"I love you, too," I said.

When I got off the phone, I was euphoric, if a bit dazed. Had I just gotten engaged? I decided to just concentrate on the fact that I now seemed to have a boyfriend I would see in two months. And I still needed that time alone.

Although some pace had returned to daily life, I was still often exhausted and distracted. I went back to teaching at the college and to ferrying Isabel around. The thought of Rich was like a lucky charm I could finger, but it wasn't a reality I could deal with immediately.

The mortuary was following me up. I didn't mind. I had liked the mortician, a pleasant Italian from a traditional family, a man not much older than I. He'd been genuinely courteous when I went in to pay by credit card, charging the cremation of my husband to Visa, where I'd be forced to see the reason for the bill one last time on my monthly statement.

So when Sister Margaret, a nun and their resident grief counselor, called, I did not resist, but made an appointment to see her. Sister Margaret was wearing the kind of clothes nuns had been wearing since they were de-habited in the seventies, skirts and thick shoes, blouses with clashing pins.

"Do you sense your husband, feel him around you?" Sister Margaret asked.

"Not really," I had to say, somewhat disappointed myself.

"Try to feel his love," she urged me.

"I don't really believe in an afterlife," I told her.

"But your husband sounds like he was so spiritual, and you're a poet!"

I shook my head.

"Whatever the forces of the universe are, I'm sure they function perfectly well without my belief," I told Sister Margaret.

"Are you sleeping?" she asked kindly.

"Not well. I have anxiety attacks in the middle of the night."

"Try to feel Robert's love around you when you wake up."

I nodded. Robert was a swell guy, but I really was not convinced that he still quote *loved* unquote me in quite such a tangible way.

"Are you eating?"

"Better," I said.

Sister Margaret was a grief counselor, well-trained; she knew our issues, we bereaved, our snacks, our vices. "Some people start drinking."

I shook my head. Sister Margaret did not seem like the person to tell what I had been smoking.

"And sex," said Sister Margaret.

Now I was paying complete attention. A nun has just said the word *sex* to me, a Jewish person. This was what it meant to be a widow; anything could happen.

"Sex," I repeated.

"Some women can't go without sex," said Sister Margaret.

And obviously I was one of them. "I have a boyfriend," I said.

"Sex can be a drug."

Thank God for that. I didn't tell Sister Margaret that I had never gone for more than two and a half months without it since I was sixteen years old, and I didn't intend to start now.

"A woman once sat in this office and told me she had to get remarried immediately so she could have sex."

"Oh."

"But I told her: Just masturbate," Sister Margaret smiled at me beatifically.

"Oh."

"How is your interest in things in general?" Sister Margaret continued the intake.

After a few more questions she studied a grief graph on her desk and informed me, "You are just at the start of your grief process. Try to feel your husband around you."

"But Sister Margaret," I protested, "I want to let him go." I had been dreaming a lot about Robert, but I didn't tell her about my dreams, unfortunately reminiscent of an Esalen encounter group, where I told the man I had loved and lived with for so many years: I can't be monogamous with you anymore; I have to date other people.

After a bit more chitchat, I thanked Sister Margaret and got up to go. She embraced me, the purposive but impersonal hug of a nun or professional.

Back out in the parking lot, I felt dazed. What had happened? I seemed set on some unusual stages of grief course, grieving through sex and drugs.

Suddenly I remembered something that Rich had told me, which had amused me. He'd seen a bumper sticker, a takeoff on the Massachusetts seat-belt campaign, which read: GRAVITY: IT'S A GOOD IDEA, AND IT'S THE LAW. Unexpectedly, I was aware of gravity, that universal law. For the first time, I understood its true purpose: to keep me stuck to the earth, crossing the asphalt, instead of flying directly up into the blue New Mexico sky, once and for all.

I was also, boyfriend or no boyfriend, functioning completely on my own. I still had affairs of Robert's to settle, and I actually kept a stack of death certificates in the car to use as needed at the bank or wherever I was concluding his business.

The largest outstanding problem was a suit against Social Security. Robert had been fired from his job with his own permission. He was basically fired for missing work because he was ill. The city's policy would have been to keep him on indefinitely on disability, but he felt oddly guilty about it. His boss also wanted and needed to fill his position, and so he told her he had no intention of returning to the job when well. This allowed her to fire him, and he lost all his benefits.

At the time, the situation enraged and terrified me. It seemed like such an irresponsible hippie thing to do. He lost his disability, and we lost our health insurance. I raged inwardly, *What did Robert expect? That I would just go on supporting us without his help?*

Apparently he was right, for that is what I did. It also frightened me that he had no intention of returning to a pleasant, parttime job that provided benefits and never interfered with his Zen duties. It seemed a sign that he did not believe he would return to health.

"I don't want them to be understaffed," was all he had said. His position of compassion had applied to his coworkers, I felt, but not to me.

As a result, he was basically penniless and began the lengthy procedure of applying for Social Security benefits. They were denied twice in a row, apparently rather programmatically.

Finally, with the help of an attorney, who was the husband of a friend of mine, Robert was given a hearing before a judge. Of course, he died before the hearing, and so I put on a demure blue dress and a small pair of turquoise earrings and set out to claim the money. Paul, our lawyer, sometimes referred to himself as Robert's last friend. Robert hadn't lived long enough for them to become old friends.

Paul and I entered the room where the judge, a Republican with a reputation for being conservative, sat with his clerk.

"Where is your client?" the judge asked, apparently having forgotten what was in the pile of papers before him.

"My client is dead, your honor," Paul said and burst into tears.

This only had a positive effect. The judge debated for less than ten minutes and awarded me the entire sum.

I was thrilled to collect almost ten thousand dollars at a time when I needed it.

It was sad, though, that Robert had never benefited. The last time he had been denied was because he was a pound over the weight limit, despite his severe weight loss from the colitis. In fact, he was eighty-four pounds when he died.

Robert and I had agreed that if we ever got a windfall, we would re-stucco the house, an expensive and dirty job that we needed to do but always put off. I paid off some bills from Korea and set about home repair on my own.

I truly realized that I was a widow the week I did two things I never would have done if my husband Robert had been alive: I went up on the roof of my own house and I got an AIDS test.

"For $1500," the roofer, Jimmy Ortiz, told me, "I can make all the repairs."

I was standing on my roof, despite my desperate fear of heights. Before the house could be properly re-stuccoed, the roof needed some patching done.

"For $750," Mr. Ortiz said, "I can do the parapets."

From the top of my roof, I could see the west side of Santa Fe stretch out towards the Jemez Mountains. The slightly shabby neighborhood looked beautiful, terraced with little yards and gardens, someplace faraway like Sicily or Spain.

My neighbor Grace came out her back door and looked up, startled, waved.

"Hello, Grace," I called.

"Hello, Mrs. C. de Baca," said Jimmy. "You have good neighbors," he told me. "I grew up in this neighborhood. They have old-fashioned values."

The AIDS test was another thing completely. I was angry about it because I knew I didn't have AIDS. But Rich had said mildly on the phone during our last conversation, "Would you please get an AIDS test or at least a note from your doctor?"

Robert, I thought, would never have said, "Mir, get an AIDS test."

Robert and I found out about AIDS together. His friend Thomas came over to our flat on Rose Alley in San Francisco's inner Fillmore to drink tea.

Thomas said, "There is a terrible new gay cancer out there on the street, and it is a CIA plot, and it is contagious, and it is going to kill us all."

We said, "Thomas, you are sooo paranoid."

Two weeks later, our neighbor Fred came down with Karposi's and started dying. It was a scene that would replay all over the city: a young guy dying, sobbing lovers, enraged friends, a dazed Italian or Irish or Mexican or anything mother from someplace utterly ordinary, like Buffalo, New York, a wake, a funeral.

If Robert were alive, he would be on the roof, not me. "I've only got $750 budgeted for this," I told Mr. Ortiz. "Just do the parapets."

"Go down the ladder a step at time," he told me in a kindly manner.

When Robert was dying, they gave him every test imaginable, including an AIDS test.

I joked, "If you are HIV negative, can I have some of that morphine?"

He must have been negative, I reasoned, because when he was in a coma, there was blood everywhere and no one seemed concerned.

But I had to do what Rich had asked. I went to the Women's Health Clinic for the test. When I went back to pick up the results, I was greeted by the nurse, Jennette, whom I knew in a mild social way.

"An AIDS test!" she exclaimed. "You don't need any more bad news, Miriam."

"What are the results?"

"But an AIDS test."

"Jenny," I said, "I have a boyfriend."

"A boyfriend!"

"My old high-school boyfriend," I said.

"Oh." She looked dreamy. "I ran into my high-school boyfriend once, and he . . ."

"What are the results?" I pleaded.

"Negative," she said.

I arranged to have the re-stucco job done during spring break, when Isabel and I would go visit Richard in Boston. I picked out a pale yellow color called "Luna." It was gorgeous, but not, I suspected, a color Robert would have agreed to. I was on my own.

Whatever nervousness I had about going to see Rich in Boston was offset by my familiarity with the city. My mother had been born there, I had lived there for eight years, and if things didn't work on the visit, I could stay at my sister Rachel's in the suburbs.

Isabel was looking forward to seeing her first cousins, and my parents had volunteered to come up from New York and baby-sit Isabel at their hotel on Friday night.

It was snowing faintly when we arrived. I'd all but forgotten that desolate dark cold that settles over New England. Rich met us at the security barrier, wearing a black beret. His hands were cold and trembling as I took them in mine.

I liked his apartment in the unfashionable area of Jamaica Plain.

"I bet this neighborhood is full of junkies and Divinity students," I said.

Rich laughed. It was a typical Boston "mixed" neighborhood.

The apartment was up one flight of stairs, which charmed Isabel, used to one-story houses. A long corridor divided the place—living, dining, and computer annex in front with bedroom and big kitchen in back. It was a bit dusty, with some piles of papers and old furniture, but it had a pleasant feeling. Not bad for a bachelor apartment. The pantry was well stocked, and Rich made us soup and toasted bagels, and added fruit and ice cream. He'd set up a bed for Isabel in the living-room alcove beneath old-fashioned windows.

"You can't sleep with Rich," she told me. "You're not married."

"Oh yes, I can," I said briskly. "Get ready for bed." And I tucked her in.

I took a bath and climbed into bed with Rich as casually as if we had been married for years. We kept waking up to make sure we were still together.

But in the morning when Rich said, "Do you want the first shower or should I?"—I almost cried. It reminded me of life with Robert when he was well. It was such a pleasure to have an ordinary exchange with a man, but it was poignant, too.

The week passed happily. I knew I must be in love because Boston, with its irritating traffic and dreadful weather, didn't even get on my nerves. We visited my sister, made love every opportunity we could get, and spent an evening at the Museum of Fine Arts, where I had been so many times with both Rich and Robert.

I said I just wanted to see the Monets; that was all. Rich said he liked Sisley. In the wide room of Impressionist paintings, some water lilies hung on the wall. I said, "Well, that was the first thing I ever cared about outside my family—Monet's water lilies."

The paintings of snow showed white on white gray—a tree, a wall. My husband was dead, and suddenly everything looked more brilliant, as if everything had a source of its own light.

I went to look at the Buddha Hall with its statues of big wooden gods and Bodhisattvas, large bodies I could depend on. Sitting in that dim hall, looking at the Buddhas—in my early twenties that had been what had awakened my interest in Buddhism, in a search for some kind of spirituality. Sitting there now, I forgot I had ever left Boston.

Rich and I shared two sandwiches for dinner at the museum cafe—one roast beef, one crab cake. He considered a glass of white wine, but didn't order it. We went home and split a bottle of beer, sipping in turn. I'd known him since I was fourteen years old, and what he knew about me wasn't all good. We made love for so long that I had to prop myself up with a hand on the floor to keep from falling off the bed.

The only melancholy note was a visit with Robert's family. His parents had come up from New Jersey, and I was touched by their effort. Robert's father had suffered a stroke a year before and was still frail. But he put out for Isabel, playing checkers, enjoying her company.

Robert's two sisters and I sat out in the motel's atrium with an indoor pool. They were obviously still in a state of extreme shock. I, of course, was doing superficially better, but we still shared the same grief. However, they were very upset about my involvement with Richard. And they took it on themselves to criticize: it was much too soon, I was in the wrong, and I had ruined Isabel's life.

"You are teaching her that people can be replaced," they announced.

I was stunned. As far as I was concerned, all I had done was acquire a boyfriend. Isabel didn't seem to mind or even notice that much.

Underneath it all was the accusation that I had betrayed Robert. I was furious. The care I had given him the last two years of his life seemed invisible to his family. The world gave me status as a widow, but the family felt its loss to be so much greater than mine, because as the sisters reiterated, "A brother can't be replaced."

We were in a competition to see whose grief was the most real. Maybe this was because during their mutually difficult teenage years Robert had been protective of his sisters, almost as if he were the parent and they, the children. Now the rule seemed to be *she who recovers first loved the least.* We would, indeed, patch things up later, but it was an excruciating moment. And I began to feel everyone judging me.

My parents arrived as promised. Isabel was delighted by the prospect of a sleepover and room service.

Rich and I had a night to ourselves, and he was giving a little party for me the next day, a brunch to meet his friends.

My father and I strolled through the Cambridge Commons in the twilight, chatting.

"I'm sort of involved with Rich," I said. I waited for my father to pounce the way Robert's sisters had, but he didn't.

My father laughed. "I'm not stupid," he said. "Why else would anyone come to Boston in March?"

I soon learned that no one over sixty—no one who had lost friends or a spouse—was remotely critical of my desire to go on with life. The older generation had also grown up at a time when early death was more common, and they took a more common-sense approach.

It was my contemporaries who were apt to be judgmental, a fact I found extremely irritating. I had been a faithful wife, and now people who were quite given to divorce and infidelity seemed to be accusing me of sluttish behavior. It took a while for me to stop being defensive.

The party in Richard's flat was exactly twenty-three years to the day after we broke up in college. It was March 16, 1996. Nine of his friends came to eat bagels and surreptitiously investigate me. I wore a short, black, silk skirt and bare feet. I felt happy to be with Rich and to be introduced to those he cared about.

In the kitchen, someone's curious boyfriend arrived late and tried to grill me.

"What is your story?" he asked.

"I won't tell you," I said, backing up.

He persisted, "What is your story, and how do you know Richard?"

I told the truth, "I am a widow. My husband was a Zen Buddhist priest. I have a seven-year-old daughter. In 1970, Richard and I lost our mutual virginity. Any more questions?"

The boyfriend looked stunned. For a moment I admired my own chutzpah and the late winter light streaming through the kitchen windows. Then I turned and went to look for Rich.

Canyon

"A year after your death
I read the journals
Of John Wesley Powell
Even this explorer
Had a boat named for his wife"

"CANYON EL GRANDE" FROM *The Widow's Coat*

After the visit to Boston, Rich and I pretty much knew that we wanted to be together. He planned to visit in May, and then Isabel and I would go and spend the summer living with him.

On the level of love, my life had taken an extraordinary—unbelievable—turn for the better.

On the level of grief, it poked along at its own pace. For the bereaved person, time is both friend and enemy. Everyone in my grief group tended to believe that the passage of time alone would heal us, but it didn't. It was as if we somehow had to work along with it. And work was the operative word. I thought about Robert all day, dreamed about him all night. My fatigue was constant.

I bought my first computer after the trip to Korea. It was distracting to have a new toy, e-mail for Kath and Rich, and a game of solitaire on the screen. I started writing a journal on it, feeling it more ephemeral than my usual bound notebook. It felt like a dream, easy to erase, but I did keep saving it.

February 6, 1996

X. told me that when it became apparent that Robert would die in the Intensive Care Unit that Y. said, "Now Isabel will have no father." Not that I wouldn't have a husband. D. said yesterday that I was so insane, it scared her. It's difficult to reconstruct things felt in a trance.

Last night I dreamed that two houses were full of ghosts—626 Kathryn and 153 Dwight Place (where I grew up).

Writing on this screen seems less real than writing on the page.

Robert has been dead 3 months and two weeks, approx. It feels like a hundred years.

Richard told me on the phone Sunday night: *I love you passionately*. I remember him so well.

I had a vision of interpenetration after Robert died. I thought the 75 people in my house were one organism. Then I thought maybe the whole human race was one organism. I think of funny things Robert used to say all day long.

February 7, 1996

Terrible dreams. The last one before waking: I get off an airplane, it's neon lit, spooky, walk past Julie and Suzi (Robert's sisters), try to pretend I don't see them. Robert is alive and they want me to get back together with him. They are very angry. I have left Isabel with Sharon or someone.

Last night at Pranzo, Hope told me she dreamed that R. looked well and healthy. She asked if he was OK being dead, and he said yes, he was fine and doing quite well.

February 8, 1996

Some melancholy housecleaning. Still trying to clear out the last of Robert's room. Threw away small, intimate stuff like his Block-buster video rental card. It's unbearable; those small arrangements of his, wondering what he was planning to do with a collection of specimen bags or a tiny screwdriver. He certainly had a lot of stuff; the room is in archaeological layers. A blank notebook I might steal. Postcards of Turner. Small things I gave him, like the Turner sketchbook. When a person dies, you get back all the gifts you gave him. Things I'll save—his odd sewing kit. The cats are in the garbage bags.

Yesterday I had lunch with A., the young dynamic widow my friends fixed me up with. She'd come from city hall, looking very chic in a peacock blue shirt. We just sat and sobbed over our pasta. (I was actually at Pranzo again!) A. and I both had fantasies we could "heal" our husbands by making love to them.

As we left, she pointed out a very Waspy, uptight couple who'd been staring at us. Apparently, they'd never seen a pair of cute widows—one Jewish, one Puerto Rican—cry at Pranzo. Too bad.

February 9, 1996

Daniel (my brother) is here! Great to see him.

We sold the JEEP. What a relief. Just took it to the Walking Man's Friend and got $2000. Not that much, but what a piece of shit that car actually was. I was very worried & then relieved. Robert's pack was in the back. I took a peek inside: his classic blue pants he always wore, green sweatshirt, green cap, and diapers. I just left it. I didn't want to ever deal with that stuff again. We had to jump the car to start it.

All the C de Baca neighbors were out and friendly as soon as Dan put in an appearance; they love him. Simon offered me his formal condolences.

Paul (our lawyer) called to say Social Security settled in our favor officially! We knew we had won, but this is good news, and more $, I think, than we'd hoped for at first, will see . . .

I'm feeling fiscally secure. The plumber and most medical are paid off, so are Korea and computer. I can take much of the summer off.

Bought my Boston tickets and sent Rich a note.

Daniel said last night he hadn't seen me like this (in love?) in fifteen years. I know less and less each day. Seeing Dan really perks me up. We sat and smoked two Camel cigarettes each and ate pistachios in the sun outside the studio.

I bought 3 gorgeous boxes at Jackalope to stash Robert's stuff I need to save.

February 11, 1996

Daniel left.

I bought 3 lace teddies and a pair of lace undies. I think about seeing Rich in Boston.

He called. I told him I was glad he wasn't here, because I was having a bad dead-person week, and he basically said he expected I'd have bad weeks about other things later, which was perceptive. He is very funny and amusing. I told him, "You are a good guy," and he said, "You are a good guy, too." Sometimes I feel more like a mess. I'm still having trouble getting things done. Richard really loves me. It's tangible to me.

The air was beautiful. Daniel and I went on a sunset drive to Tesuque. Isabel sobbed and asked how the police would know to come if I were dead. We talked about dialing 911, about Hope being her guardian, and that I won't die.

I talked to S. He was unutterably sweet. His daughter died as a newborn. I asked: How did you manage? He said, "I'm a guy. I swept it under the rug." He told me, "You won't die." I said, "This sucks," and he laughed a lot and said that I have a good attitude.

February 12, 1996

Monday. I had a perfectly pleasant day. Hope said I seemed full of energy. I took Isabel to school, taught, went out for Chinese food, shopped, taught a private, did some troubleshooting on the phone, picked up Reuben, then Isabel, saw Hope and Pearl, made valentines with Isabel, talked to Sharon. I don't know . . . it was a normal day, maybe the first since Robert died.

I got a package and a nice letter from Richard; saving the package until Valentine's Day.

I think about Robert, how our destinies have diverged, how I can't do anything for him anymore or ever again. It's odd, I miss his body the least of all. But I still want to talk to him. I guess I know his body is gone.

Did I mention that a few days ago I bought into the Jewish Burial Society plots? I bought 1 and a half plots, thinking, I guess, 2–3 people could rest there, cremated. I must be thinking of remarrying.

Sharon said, "Have you noticed that some women ALWAYS have men, and we are those women?" I have noticed. It alarms me a bit, but it just seems true. Is it that I can't be alone? I'd rather look at it positively.

February 14, 1996

A warm pleasant day. Rich sent me & Isabel a great Valentine's box—two kinds of candy and handmade valentines.

Last night I pretty much finished sorting Robert's stuff. Can't find the notebook with the stuff we were working on when he died: his piece, "I want a canoe and the strength to use it." I suspect someone or other of lifting it, but like anything of his that goes lost or missing, I imagine it must all be for the best.

Still, I want to record some of his stuff. He wrote down a devastating sonnet, presumably Shakespeare, (found it later—140) about sickness and death.

Things Robert gave me:

a dwarf papyrus plant

2 zebra finches

2 green male parakeets

a pair of green jade Buddha earrings

flowers

red licorice

a jade-colored celadon teacup

a large paste-jewel pin, shaped like a strawberry

never perfume, underwear, or any article of clothing, no
    hat, gloves

no blank notebooks

a picture of 19th-century Egypt, painted on glass

where the hell are his Eno cars that I wanted but he'd
    never give???

a major arcana, Bota deck

books

a strangely shaped mushroom

a carrot with two legs

green paper umbrella

stamps

In Robert's notebook, as early as August 31, 1993: "gut full of worms."

Was he sick the whole time I knew him, his whole adult life? Why didn't I NOTICE more profoundly. Did I? I find few clues in my own writing before 1994.

Again, from R. presumably 1993: "Death is no longer funny. M & I talking & laughing late at night. In the age of AIDS, death is no longer funny. People talk as if death is no longer funny. The lips of the dead move in their graves when you read their portion. (This must be some kabalistic info from me via my Hebrew teacher Yehudis) It's so hard to say good-bye to someone whose life has bent yours. I'll never really understand that certain people are really dead. What can you really do for the dead except say good-bye, take care, dissolve, don't suffer."

February 18, 1996

I talked to Rich for almost two hours again last night. It seems we basically agreed to get married. I was sweating so hard that I had to change my shirt afterwards. The whole thing is terrifying. I felt mad—at him, at Robert, at having to negotiate.

Today, Joanna said to me, "You are in love." I know I am. I am meant to be with him. But how can this be so soon after Robert's death?

On some level, I don't care at all. Karma is karma, I'm on a roll, I'm going somewhere, I don't know where.

Things that Robert liked:

the song "Baby, Please Don't Go"
teacups

Nova Scotia salmon

women

world beat music

extremely tedious serial music

deciduous trees

Isabel

bookstores

trashy science fiction

space travel

astronauts

weddings

maps

office supplies

fish prints

silence

knowing painters

formality

extension cords

rice-paper lamps

Things I agreed with Robert about:

AIDS

adultery

linoleum

Chilmark, Martha's Vineyard in the winter being better
    than the summer

the New Age

German Zen students

Japanese things being beautiful
living intentionally
abortions

Things I disagreed with Robert about:

the color to paint the house
dogs
T.S. Eliot
money
astrology, Tarot, holistic healing
haiku (he scorned it)
Zionism (he was pro)
how to drive
language school poets
clothes

February 26, 1996

What am I supposed to do about my slight alienation from everyone? Y. says I seem hyper. X. says our lives are totally different. I know I am totally different in some way, but it upsets me when my friends feel the separation. I guess I'm afraid they won't love me any more. I think I must have looked very straight before Robert died.

Dee—Dee, of all people!—said she was shocked to hear about Richard.

I am alone in all this, but I was also alone before, profoundly alone when Robert was sick, and I've always felt alone as an artist.

Then I asked X. to dinner and she cheered up. I know I need to stop pleasing people, and yet

... and yet ...

March 6, 1996

Computer makes odd beeping noises.

Therapy. Sob.

X. looks incredulous every time I mention Rich.

WHERE IS ROBERT??? Where did he GO? I sob and tell my therapist Fred, "I don't have a story for this; I don't have a narrative." He says, "You will." Somehow I believe him. I think about Robert. I look at the fountain in the courtyard of the community college. I think, *Robert is dead.* I think, *I'm in love with Richard.* I think, *I don't give a fuck that Robert is dead.* But I miss him. Certain things I'll never have again, but sex certainly isn't one of them, or love. But the poetry connect. The words *bass line.*

How come Rich isn't more worried about my dead husband?

It's easy to shock people. The psychic at the Purim fair told me to give up the Scheherazade routine, the dance of the seven veils. Total PMS. Why I don't make sense to other people anymore.

Where the fuck is Kath when I need her?

Julie called to say Ben is dead (painter friend with a brain tumor in NYC). How this wouldn't have upset Robert. How it does not upset me. How you can turn this into a thing, a death trip if you will.

How it irritates me that X. says Y. has had so much loss! What about me? WHAT ABOUT ISABEL???

Questions to ask Robert:

Where are the Eno cards?
What color stucco?
Can Isabel go to Harvard?
Did you secretly think I was fat?
Did you forgive me?
Could you hear in the coma?
Where is the notebook?
What's under the rock?
Were you always sick?
Did you mind?
Are you OK?
Where is Issan?
Are you glad X. is going to marry Y.?
Where is your thighbone?
Will I see you again?

March 29, 1996

Ana says, "No one knows how much you suffered, Miriam. You didn't say, and besides, no one ever knows about somebody else."

We ate gumbo on the terrace of Celebrations restaurant, and it SNOWED on us!

April 6, 1996

Yesterday I had to tell the UPS man than Robert was dead. It was the young guy Robert knew dimly from the library whose godparents were the Luceros, who used to live across the street.

This morning I danced to a tape Robert had made for me— "There Goes My Baby," that old Donna Summer song. I started crying. Where is he? It's easier to be faithful to a living person than a dead one.

April 9, 1996

Very bad dream. Robert has been in prison for several years. He was set up with some gangsters, but was also at fault for being very violent. Now he is coming out of prison, but I don't want him to live with us, I want Richard. Confusion about Isabel custody, also anxiety that Robert will get a girlfriend who will not be an appropriate stepmother.

April 18, 1996

Windy day. Peach tree in bloom. Only two more easy weeks to the semester.

Grief group. Not much to say. Am I losing my grip on grief? Some people in my group seem more crazy than grief-stricken.

Something that I REALLY wanted to tell Robert: that the Ned Rothenberg, who is a famous avant-garde saxophonist, really IS the Ned I went to summer camp with. Paul told me.

Why did I tell Rich, after going to bed with him for the first time in 23 years, that Chaco has 400 miles of paved road? Because I wanted him to know what I know. I miss that with Robert.

April 26, 1996

Enormous forest fire in the Jemez. Huge cloud of smoke over our house, literally blocking out the sun, which shines as a RED disc high in the sky, 5:50 P.M. Very frightening, and I rather wish I was not alone. Called the forest service. It is west of Bandelier, so on the other side of the Rio, but I'm sort of worrying about all that smoke.

My birthday tomorrow & Robert's the next day. Just trying to get through it.

May 5, 1996

I did something tonight I never did before: smoked an unfiltered Camel cigarette by myself. It was bliss. I sat on the floor.

Robert has been dead 6 ½ months.

Today Isabel told her Hebrew school class about his death. She cried a lot about him last night. And wrote on the computer, "We were a happy family until I was six, and my dad died." That isn't quite true, of course.

Took a walk. Lots of lilacs. Wrote a little. Small things. I can't really handle much more. I bought three notebooks at Toys R Us and started keeping a journal in the pink one. I think sometimes for hours about bad things Robert did to me—and hold a grudge—much as I loved him.

Does it help me to write? Not exactly. But it doesn't help not to.

When will I come out of this cocoon of widowhood?

My boyfriend Richard arrives in less than 48 hours.

This is the first night in a week I've been able to stay awake past 9 P.M. I realize I'm no longer capable of desperate acts the way I was right after Robert died.

May 21, 1996

Grand Canyon, AZ

My father says accurately, "You are living in two worlds at the same time."

It's so odd to think about all the things Robert will never see or experience.

Hour alone on the south rim of the Grand Canyon. Just sitting and looking, cry. Robert is dead, why can't I wrap my mind completely around this? Why do I feel I have to change, but not know how.

May 22, 1996

A point of contact between the spirit and the human world—a limestone sink hole, a hot spring. Your eyes, suddenly startled, open in pleasure.

Last night I actually dreamed I was eating Robert's ashes, and they were full of licorice pieces.

May 23, 1996

Changed the message on my phone machine. It has my voice on it for the first time since Robert died.

Talked to T. I wish she'd stop saying she wished someone else had died instead of Robert, *why him*, etc. as if death were a contest rather than inevitable.

I realized how sexist it is for anyone to expect that a widow won't recover. I did shock some people with Rich. Good. A year from now, no one will care.

The incredible freaky thing that T. said to me on the phone: she'd decided Robert had turned 37 on his birthday, and he was still older than she. It's scary.

It can take me all day to get a medium amount of work done.

May 27, 1996

Rain! Cold, overcast day. Merciful rain. Cranky again, that feeling that things are not all right, and of course, they aren't with Robert dead.

Last night I dreamed about Lewis (college boyfriend). We were back at Harvard, but it was the present; he was married, and I, widowed. He gave me lots of drugs, which I was trying to flush down a disgusting toilet. I hugged him, somehow knowing we wouldn't be together sexually, and said, "I just want you to know I love you."

The spring after Robert died was in many ways a peaceful, even healing, time. I lived alone with my daughter, but I knew that it was time limited. I was in a quiet limbo state, making my own decisions, pleasing no one.

All spring, terrible forest fires raged across New Mexico. Just behind Los Alamos, acres of forest burned in the Jemez Mountains. The rage of the elements made me miss Robert. He would have loved the forest fire, despite its destructive power. I could hear his voice in my head, criticizing the way the Forest Service handled fire, not allowing smaller fires to burn unchecked, until the mess of undergrowth finally caused an out-of-control conflagration.

Robert knew a lot about many things and a little about practically everything. Every time I rushed onto the front porch to watch the smoke black out an angry red sun, I thought of him, and his knowledge of forests, and how certain trees needed fire to have their seeds grow.

One thing I did with my solitude was to watch videos. I had always been embarrassed to watch schmaltzy things when Robert was around to tease me, so now I indulged. I watched every widow movie I could find. They helped the tears flow, but they also helped with self-definition. Who was I? What had happened to me? Did anyone share my perceptions? The word widow means "empty," the dictionary informed me. I had been uneasy at first with the word "wife." When I had first married Robert, I didn't want my identity reduced, although I soon realized my fears were quite exaggerated. But I liked the word widow. I had changed completely. I was glad my label had changed.

I saw *Truly, Madly, Deeply*, which was my favorite. I loved how the heroine's dead boyfriend came back as a ghost to live with her until she started two-timing him with someone living. I loved how he found the apartment too cold and how his weird dead friends seemed to be Eastern European classical musicians. I watched it and sobbed. I also felt I was unfaithful to a dead man.

Donia Flor and Her Two Husbands was the flip, a sexy dead husband comes back to console the wife. When I told Rich I had seen it, he fretted that he was in the position of the uptight second husband. These movies relieved me, though, with their dead men so real they could be conjured at will and with women with sex on their minds, trying to move on.

The French classic, *A Man and a Woman*, was easy to take with a bucket of tears, but Hollywood offered less. *Sleepless In Seattle* and *Ghost* had no emotional content for me, because they didn't really seem to deal with death.

A writer friend with whom I shared a taste in old black-and-white movies left a copy of *The Ghost and Mrs. Muir*, the original movie with Gene Tierney. It was perplexing thematically; a woman is widowed only to be visited by someone else's ghost, an old sea captain who dictates his memoirs and makes her a famous writer. Things seemed curiously displaced, but I didn't mind watching Gene Tierney.

Beyond Rangoon was the best of the American lot, because the widow immediately wanted to be somewhere faraway, extreme, violent, and where people were suffering. I knew the feeling.

The books I read were less help. I was still searching, trying to place my experience. Surely being widowed was a common and ordinary thing. But there weren't many models around me. There was only one of a young widow in my own family.

I remembered when my cousin Sam died and left his wife Myrtle a widow. I must have been about ten years old. It was just around the time that the surgeon general's report came out on cigarettes causing lung cancer, and as if on cue, Sam got a terrible pain in his back, which turned out to be a tumor, and he died.

Sam was notorious as an unfaithful husband. His famous remark, which my father once repeated to me after two beers, was, "It's not infidelity if you can't get it at home." My brother and I spent many happy hours laughing over this and trying to figure out exactly what Sam couldn't get, but of course at that time it was serious family business. Sam had a mistress in Manhattan, and my grandfather, his boss, advised Myrtle to start driving in from Jersey against traffic to pick Sam up every evening at six sharp.

Apparently, the problem had started on their honeymoon. My father knew this because he had been *on* that honeymoon. It was the height of the great depression, and as a treat, my grandmother drove Sam and Myrtle from New York to Florida. My father and his younger brother came along. No wonder there was a problem with the honeymoon that had three other people on it. Sam died. My cousin Myrtle became what I know of widows. She was forty-two and a grandmother. Her greatest goal in life was to keep her kitchen floor clean. I once dropped a spotless apple on that spotless floor, and she tried to throw it out until my mother, who couldn't bear to waste food, stepped in and let me eat it.

Myrtle did not seem like a role model. She had died of poorly treated diabetes just five years after Sam.

I made a list of other widows so I wouldn't feel so anomalous.

Rock and Roll:

> Yoko Ono
> Courtney Love
> Patti Smith

Literary:

> Madame Max
> Wife of Bath
> Fermina Daza

Classic:

> Coretta King
> Jackie Kennedy
> Elizabeth Taylor

Historical:

> Mary Shelley
> Kate Chopin

I tried to imagine what my life would be like now if I had never left New Jersey. I wrote in my diary:

New Jersey Widow: An Alternate Life

I am forty-two years old. I live with my parents and my young daughter in the house I grew up in in New Jersey. Every morning I put on my tight black suit and go to work as a book-keeper in my father's cousin's company. My father's cousin runs a trucking company, a business that is notoriously corrupt. I walk into my office, take off my suit jacket, and hang it on the back on the chair so it won't get wrinkled. I arrive at 8:15 A.M. and leave by 3:20 P.M. so I can pick up my daughter at school. She comes running down the hill with a pink lunch box. We go home to my parents' quiet house. My father is retired, and he breeds rare orchids. My mother still works in the tailoring shop.

Every Friday and Saturday night I go out with a different man. I am set up constantly by my cousins, my boss, the foreman at work, and the people I went to high school with. I let these men take me to nice family-style Italian or Armenian restaurants, Jewish delis, fancy Greek diners. We go to the movies or dancing in a club. We would no more venture into Manhattan than to the moon.

The problem is, I begin to lie. I say my husband drowned racing a yacht across the Atlantic. I say he died of AIDS-like symptoms that probably weren't AIDS. I say I loved him so passionately that I threw myself into the open grave. Most of these men do not ask me out a second time. They are heavyset, New Jersey men in their forties and fifties. Some wear gold pinkie rings. Some are divorced. There seems to be an endless supply of them.

On Sunday night, I stay home.

The vision terrified me, even as I amused myself with it. I was glad to be who I was, where I was, if bereaved.

My solitude was punctuated by a small trip. My father, still looking out for us, took us on a memorable jaunt to Arizona. We met him in Phoenix and stayed at the luxurious Biltmore, a

Mayan Deco hotel designed by Frank Lloyd Wright. We spent all day soaking and swimming in one of the numerous swimming pools, with Isabel shrieking down the water slide.

But I could see he was still quite worried about us. Isabel often sobbed violently before bedtime, and my father heard her through the hotel wall. What was common to me—a child still distraught with a grief I could keep company but in no way fix— was a frightening sight and sound to those outside our reality.

We took the long dusty drive to the Grand Canyon and slept on the rim. My father and I had hiked down the canyon when I was in my twenties and he less than a decade older than I was now. I had never been there with Robert.

I sat on the rim and looked out into a vastness that rivaled any other view on earth. In the early morning light the pale oranges and soft purples of the stones had the depth of an ocean. Far below, what I could see from where I sat, the river was continuing to cut its way into the earth. Maybe on that river, rafts were plunging down white water, the rafters too tiny to imagine from this height. I smelled piñon in the heat of the day and far off, a whiff of burning. A blue jay scolded along the underbrush. The stone wall of the canyon shimmered as the sun began to heat. Like grief, the canyon was laid down in alluvial levels—the most recent level on the top.

More forest fires raged around the canyon. We drove out of our way to avoid road closures caused by them. If fire and destruction in the outer world mirrored something inside me, I was also longing for another element. It was time, for the first time since Robert had died, to go look at the ocean.

Ocean

"In our story
It is the wife and child
Who remain
Left with the bookcase you made
Of driftwood
Saving your paperweight—
A red brick smoothed by waves."

"MILKY WAY" FROM *Archeology of Desire*

In the middle of June, eight months after Robert died, Isabel and
I moved to Boston to live with Rich for the summer. It was a kind
of a trial period, but one that we felt sure would work out. And if
it did, then Rich would relocate to Santa Fe to live with us.

Before we left, I readied the house for its sitter, who had been
instructed to let our kitties come and go, inside and out, as they
pleased for the first time. Isabel and I had been too worried about
them before, but now, it seemed time for them to become outdoor
cats, particularly if we didn't have to watch and worry during the
transition.

I also went to the dermatologist to have a suspicious-looking spot taken off my face. The doctor seemed quite clear that it was cancer, the noninvasive basal cell carcinoma. It ran in my family, and there was a high rate in sun-scorched Santa Fe.

Still, the word cancer gave me frightening pause. After Robert had died, I was sure I would get some kind of terrible disease. I had heard the word cancer over and over in my head until I was convinced I would soon be terminally ill. Was this it?

The dermatologist assured me it was simple to remove—should the biopsy show cancer—and so slow-growing that I was welcome to put the tiny operation off until fall. I trusted him, not only because he had been my doctor for years but because in a former life he had been a California surfer and apparently had had literally dozens of such skin cancers taken off his back.

"Just use sunscreen at the beach," he said, "and have a good time. Life's too short!" He was obviously unaware of my recent history; still, the advice was good.

I wrote in my journal:

June 13, 1996

I was lonelier when Robert was sick than I am now.

Cenotaph—the monument you erect to what is empty.

J.'s grief is a fixed thing. But nothing is fixed in this floating world. This world that floats. Flame boats on the water. Petals.

I have actually had many happy times since Robert died, particularly of late.

June 21, 1996

Albuquerque airport to Logan, to live with Rich in Boston for
eight weeks. It seems I just spent the last few days sobbing. My
therapist Fred said, "Don't take Robert with you." I think I look
OK—flowered dress, black shoes.

Will I have fun? Will my skin cancer be OK? Will I get married? Will my career take off? Will I inherit money?

If a memorial is by its nature empty . . .

It was oddly familiar to be spending the summer in Boston, a
city I had lived in for eight years of my life. Rich and I had actually lived together for a summer there almost twenty-five years
before, the summer I graduated from high school. I was going to
Harvard summer school before starting as a freshman, and Rich
had a summer job and was learning to drive.

What I remembered of that summer was the stifling heat, the
thickness of green trees, the freedom to sleep with him every
night. I was taking a botany class and carefully set up a coleus
plant so I could observe its breathing and collected and drew various seaweeds from the shore. I took a government class, too,
taught by a nasty and reactionary professor, who was a rude intro-
duction to higher education.

"There are no untormented geniuses," he announced one
day in class, apropos of not much.

One cute guy put up his hand and said, "But there are: Bach,
Picasso, and Miles Davis." Of course, Miles Davis was no happy
man. But the statement was an opening on a bigger world.

Still, the sublet apartment Rich and I had shared had been cluttered and a little depressing, full of the random possessions of other students. My sense of joy of having escaped the confines of my family and having entered the adult world had been mixed with an ineffable sense of loneliness and dislocation. I had found dorm life to be an immature relief that fall.

In some odd dreamy way, this summer felt connected to the first. Both summers shared an apartment with fans going, buses and subways, Richard's cooking, and a sense of solitude and enclosure.

However, despite my grief, or perhaps because of it, I felt acutely alive the summer in Jamaica Plain. We soon fell into a pleasant domestic routine.

I had never spent two whole months with Isabel without working. Even when she was an infant, I had been freelancing and dashing out the door to teach some class or other. She had never spent a summer home without day camp. Now we had nothing much to do but hang out together.

In many ways, that summer represented our real healing from Robert's death. In part, this was due to having leisure.

Our society does not really allow the bereaved much time in which to heal. If a spouse or child dies, most people take a few days off, a few weeks at most, then go back to work. People take off even less time for the death of a parent or sibling.

I was no different. I felt a responsibility to my students, I didn't want to lose my job, and I needed the money. I missed four days of work, in all. And people kept encouraging me to use work as a way to distract myself.

My father had told me about one of his employees when he was still in the garment industry, a Mr. Stutzl. Mr. Stutzl's wife had died slowly and horribly of brain cancer, and he had told my father, "If it weren't for coming to work every morning, I should have gone mad."

But it wasn't distraction that I needed. I had needed that when Robert was ill, and I had wanted to keep myself firmly planted in the world of practical realities. Like Mr. Stutzl, work had helped me keep going.

Now grief had propelled me into a different world. Months later, I finally had the leisure to grieve more completely. Rich was a great support, so I wasn't afraid of falling into the depression of complete solitude. I also could dedicate myself to my daughter.

Richard's apartment also had no working television or VCR. We needed to entertain ourselves. I had bought more than a hundred dollars worth of Lego kits, complicated ones of pirate ships and rockets. Isabel spread out the pieces on the living room floor and spent days assembling them.

Right across the street was a decrepit little grocery store where Rich bought his morning *Boston Globe*. Isabel and I slept late, waking after eight just as he was leaving. We'd go to the store too; I'd buy my morning cup of coffee, and Isabel would put a quarter in a machine and receive a costume jewelry ring in a bubble pack.

The store was owned by two enormous ladies, one black, one white, unusual in a neighborhood famous for its racial tension. They had a VCR with a screen mounted high on the wall that played fabulous vintage musical comedies all day long. Isabel and

I would stand transfixed for a routine from *Flower Drum Song* or *The King and I*.

The white lady would shake her head and caution Isabel to stop wasting her money on the rings. But Isabel collected them and then spread them on the rug in an elaborate mosaic game that would absorb her for hours.

To Rich's horror, I sometimes bought an egg salad sandwich or a pickle from the store—although we had the same things at home—just for the pleasure of it. I enjoyed the small treat of take-out, wrapped in thick white paper.

"We're from New Mexico," I told the lady, "but we're spending the summer with my boyfriend, the guy who comes in for the paper." She nodded in recognition and exclaimed, "New Mexico! You see many people out that way?" Obviously, she was visualizing us in a lonely farmstead with a desolate windmill turning against a huge sky.

But even compared to Santa Fe, Boston was exciting. Most days Isabel and I ventured the few blocks to the T and took the orange line into town. She learned to navigate around junkies and to take an elevator that smelled of piss—two more novelties. We'd go downtown and visit the Science Museum or the Children's Museum or blow our budget at FAO Schwartz.

On Mondays, we went to the movies; the cold air-conditioning of the matinee and the peaceful darkness in which nothing was required of us brought back my own childhood memories.

At least once a week we'd go out to my sister's house in the suburbs. Rachel's children, Max and Sophie, were a few years younger than Isabel, and they mutually doted on each other.

Swimming in the cold, murky, green lake with my sister and the children, I was transported back in time. I might have been a fifties' mother, unemployed, unworried. We'd buy ice cream cones and sit at redwood tables, watching the flock of Canada geese that meandered along the shore. The air smelled of sunscreen and hot dogs. The slight boredom of it all was reassuring after the storm we had passed through.

Rich would come home around six thirty and make supper for us all. He didn't expect me to cook, and I didn't offer. I felt taken care of in that hot, dusty apartment with the sounds of the street and the neighbors coming through the windows. Classical music played quietly on the radio. He'd read to Isabel, build forts with her out of the couch cushions, play a game or two, and I'd put her to bed. We'd make love intensely, our mood shifting from gentle to wild and back.

However, I still dreamed constantly of Robert. I would awaken at the hour of the wolf with my heart pounding, get up, crawl over Rich from my spot between his body and the wall, navigate to the bathroom, and try to get back to sleep.

In general, though, I felt better physically than I had at any other point since Robert had become ill. The feeling tone was more complicated, though. Sometimes I missed Robert, just from something simple like seeing a tin of hard candies he liked. I felt almost guilty eating them alone.

Robert's sister Julie lived in Boston, and we saw her often. Despite her initial reaction to my affair with Rich, she was an accepting person in her own way and a dedicated aunt. Isabel and I had lunch with her in Chinatown, and then browsed the curio stores. An old man rubbed Isabel's cheeks and exclaimed over them the way everyone had in Korea. Isabel slept often at Julie's, giving Richard and me time alone. One time she came home from Julie's toting an enormous, stuffed Bugs Bunny, half her size, bought by her indulgent aunt.

That evening, as she hugged Richard before bed, Isabel asked in very imperious tone, "Do you love me?"

And he said in a considered way, "I do love you."

We went to various festivities and parties, visiting with Rich's friends, who were curious to meet us. One weekend we went to a barbecue in Braintree; it was the town's anniversary holiday, complete with their special custom of illuminating the lake. This illumination was a labor-intensive event, requiring people to set up pink flares at short intervals around the entire perimeter of the town's lake. Flags and bunting hung on the main street; the smell of hot dogs permeated the air. I felt far from New Mexico in this quintessentially New England setting.

Then I saw it. A huge, man-sized skeleton, standing in the hallway of our host's house. A Day of the Dead skeleton, grinning broadly with all its teeth, wearing a large, black, felt sombrero and a serape, in a parody of a Grateful Dead album cover. I blinked, it was gone, an obvious hallucination that no one else could see.

Later that night, sitting on the sand of the town beach, watching the pink flares outline the lake and later watching fireworks explode their golden blossoms across the sky, I admitted my own alienation. I might eat hamburgers, smile and laugh in public, but privately I was still wandering in two worlds, crossing between the living and the dead.

My parents had a house in the town of Chilmark on the island of Martha's Vineyard. They tended to protect their summer privacy vigorously, which wasn't easy, considering they had four children with families lined up to visit.

Still, Robert and I had spent a lot of time there. We had once lived there for the better part of six months, watching the soft spring of songbirds and pale wildflowers come to the harsh environment of a barrier island in the Atlantic. When I had left, it was in a cold November wind, scattering the last brown oak leaves, while three, large black rooks cawed indignantly as I packed my car well past the time when they thought the house should be theirs.

When Isabel was about a year old, we managed a two-month vacation there, off-season again. A smallish whale had died and washed onto our stony beach. Robert was fascinated by it, paying it daily visits, watching the flesh deteriorate. He had a naturalist's curiosity, but he visited the remains of the great sea mammal with the friendly compassion of a Zen priest.

I wanted to go back to Chilmark, of course, but I dreaded the familiar scene without Robert.

The journey from Boston, which I had taken so many times over the course of my life, was a ritual all its own. Isabel and I took the orange line, changed to the red line, walked through South Station, which was now re-gentrified beyond recognition, crossed the train platforms, and took an elevator up to the bus station. All the way, we were lugging our suitcases in the humid Boston heat. The mere feeling of the strap of my bag cutting into my shoulder brought back so many similar starts of journeys.

The bus was usually pleasant—not too crowded on a weekday—and air-conditioned. This time there was enough room for each of us to take a window seat, Isabel sitting across the aisle from me. The trip was so familiar, but thrilling, pulling out of urban grime, taking the loop past the suburbs.

I always looked out for the oil tank painted by Corita, the abstract expressionist who was also a nun. She had draped the three-dimensional canvas with huge splashes of color. If you looked carefully at the blue splash, there was the unmistakable profile of Ho Chi Minh. Legend had it, she had painted it there on purpose during the height of the Viet Nam War. Then again, it may have been coincidence.

We crossed the WPA-era bridge that spanned the Cape Cod canal and headed down the Cape itself to Wood's Hole, past the old, white clapboard houses flanked in orange lilies. Wood's Hole with the ferry was always a preview of the island—brilliant blue bay, gulls, smell of the sea. There were more unloading and dragging of luggage until we found ourselves a seat on the ferry and settled in.

On the top deck, it was a traditional sport to hold out a treat, like a potato chip or piece of sandwich bread, for the gulls that followed the ferry. Isabel held a chip aloft until one greedy gull swooped down and snatched it roughly from her hand.

It was windy on top, and we held on to our hats. I watched a group of tourists speaking Italian. In chic sports clothes, they laughed and snacked, a bunch of middle-aged people obviously enjoying themselves. They knew nothing about death, about suffering, I told myself. Yet they were doomed to learn.

Then I had some odd thoughts. What if they did know and were enjoying themselves anyway? What if life, in its own way, was as strong as death?

This was a novel thought for me and not just because of Robert. When I was twenty-one and living in Boston, I had had a near-death experience, which was to mark me forever. It started as a bad flu, which was misdiagnosed at a big city hospital. I went to the emergency room with an acute pain in my right side, was told it was muscle pain from the fever, and was sent home with Valium. What I actually had was "devil's grip" pleurisy.

As days passed, my right lung filled with fluid and my left collapsed. When I was finally admitted to the Beth Israel Hospital, I had a high fever, a raging infection, reduced lung capacity, and no diagnosis. A surgeon opened my chest, inserted tubes to drain it, and I was put on intravenous antibiotics and placed in the intensive care unit on a series of machines. My frantic parents were told the prognosis was not good; I would probably die.

In the ICU for over a week, I soon developed something called "sleep deprivation psychosis." I was on morphine for the pain, drifting in and out of consciousness. There, I had a series of what I assumed were hallucinations. I saw my soul leave my chest; my point of view changed as I looked down at my prone body beneath me. I saw gates open and light flood out. I came to a thick black line and was about to cross when something inside warned me to turn back.

Then my body rallied. I spent almost two more months in the hospital, recovering from the surgery, which has scarred a quarter of my torso.

The eventual diagnosis was empyema, a nineteenth-century disease that flooded the lung with anaerobic organisms and killed the patient. It had been difficult to diagnose because it was so rarely seen after the invention of antibiotics.

I recovered physically, although the pain along the scar and in the bottom of my right lung remained acute for almost twenty years, when I finally overcame it through physical and emotional therapies.

The pain had been unrelenting and distorting. I felt completely betrayed by my body. Much more upsetting, however, were the experiences in the ICU. In my secular family, I had no vocabulary for what had happened. Even if I had, no one would have listened. I had no map to explain that my soul had left my body. This was several years before Kubler-Ross's work appeared in print, and accounts of near-death experiences became commonplace. Mine had been a classic, but I had no idea what had happened.

My life was saved in the Beth Israel Hospital in Boston, but in another way, it was over. I would never be the person I had been. My awareness of death became acute, which in some ways was good, as it kept me from living in ways that were inauthentic for me. The sense that life was fragile motivated me continually after my surgery. But I was haunted by the sensation that I had somehow died, and then been yanked, almost unwillingly, back to life like an errant helium balloon tugged by the string.

There, on the ferry, listening to the tourists speak Italian, I wondered if in some way I hadn't overestimated death. I was still alive, despite everything, and my life might not even be half over.

At the beach, Isabel and I enjoyed ourselves with my parents, doing familiar things, going to familiar places. The house was airy and uncluttered, open to the ocean breeze that flowed on all but the hottest days.

The first sight of the Atlantic was a bit of a shock, though. I walked, as always, through pine scrub and oak, looking for the delicate Indian pipe that sometimes grew, white fungus in the sandy soil. Then I reached the small dunes behind the rocky beach, crossed them, and saw the brilliant blue waves against a paler sky.

"Robert's dead," I told the Atlantic Ocean, as if it were a person who needed to know.

But soon the rhythm of beach life took over.

June 26, 1996

Went to the beach this morning, much too cold to swim, but Isabel ran in and out of the spray like a sandpiper.

Twenty heart-pounding, dreadful minutes waiting for the dermatologist's report. It is just a little basal cell carcinoma, which I can have out in August. But here I am praying that it is basal cell, not something worse, when before I was praying it would be normal, and now I'm relieved. The mind is impossible, a trapped rat.

I saw yesterday something odd about reality; that life and death really are quite separate. For twenty years, between my lung surgery and Robert's death, I thought we should be aware of death, preparing for it. Now I see the two states as utterly different.

Looking at all the people on the ferry reminded me life is just heedless, that is its nature.

I remember a dozen years ago Carol Rankin visiting this beach house. She was dying of brain cancer, but read Vogue, ate pasta, walked on the beach with her new boyfriend, who was our old friend. She seemed so alive—a Zen priest—and yet at the time, I was shocked that she behaved so mundanely. Now I'm closer to understanding.

June 27, 1996

Not much. Beach day. Walked on Squibnocket with my father, egg salad at the Galley, found a large starfish, and brought it home to dry. My father and Isabel flying their pirate kite on the beach. The general reading and napping and puttering of my family. Mailed six postcards. Robert is dead. I'm not. The starfish has a red pebble embedded in it.

June 28, 1996

Ants got my starfish, and I ended up tossing it into the woods behind the house that are turning to oak because of the pine-borers.

Back in Boston. Trekked back yesterday. Walked out to shop with Isabel in the green, humid, Boston neighborhood, and made dinner, which felt good, and Rich ate it.

July fourth came around, which was actually the anniversary of the first time Rich and I had kissed—when I was fifteen, and he was sixteen. It had been his very first kiss. This time his parents, people who hadn't seen me since I was eighteen years old, were in town. We were a little nervous going to meet them at their motel and then off to a game of miniature golf.

Isabel had taken her big Bugs Bunny along for the ride, fastened into the seatbelt next to hers.

"Please leave Bugs in the car," Rich said.

"Why?"

"My parents are kind of old, and they are meeting you for the first time. They might not like Bugs."

"Not like Bugs?"

Two very familiar, if older, people came towards me, waving excitedly.

Richard's mother won my regard by saying immediately, "I am so sorry about your husband." It was a kind thing to say, as I was now practically engaged to the middle-aged son she so desperately wanted to see married.

But Richard's father endeared himself to Isabel. "Bugs Bunny!" he exclaimed. "Is he coming with us to play miniature golf?"

Isabel looked startled at this change of presumed attitude. "Can he?"

"Sure! Bring him along!"

Rich and I had always shared a liking for miniature golf. At the course off Route 9, Isabel liked the patriotic themes of each hole, which were appropriate to the holiday celebrating the Revolutionary War. One thing I liked about mini-golf was that it always felt like a kind of maze. You worked your way through methodically, predictably coming to the end. It was both like and unlike life itself.

Back at the motel, Rich and Isabel played rambunctiously in the pool.

"Excuse me," Rich's mother said, "for this odd question. But did your late husband look like Richard? Because Richard and Isabel look a lot alike."

"Yes," I admitted, "Robert and Richard are of a type." Rich did look like Isabel's father, leaping around in the pool.

The summer passed gently along. The first time my sister Rachel walked into Rich's Jamaica Plain apartment she did a double take. "Is this your alternate life? Have you been living here in Boston for the last twenty years?"

There was a dreamy sense of the threads of my life hooking up together and weaving a new pattern. The surface of my life was pleasant, although my unconscious mind was still deeply troubled.

But things were changing. I even had to give up some of the vices I had taken up when Robert died.

July 3, 1996

Isabel caught me smoking a filtered cigarette on the back porch and sobbed until I promised to quit.

July 5, 1996

Bad dreams about Robert—he is in a coma, comes out of it, looking very bruised and yellow. Somehow trying to take care of him and get him to a doctor. A sorrowful feeling.

Isabel working on a set of wooden models I bought. I did laundry, mopped floor, talked on the phone.

Transparencies of time, one over the other. How much I did love Robert!

July 10, 1996

These days, waking up, I don't know who or where I am, a confusion. Robert is still dead.

I feel myself grow close to Richard, warm.

Took the T to FAO Schwartz, which truly impresses Isabel. She cashes in her 100 points (for good behavior) for a glorious butterfly Barbie doll.

Today I felt my own strength, how tough I really am, how it would take a hell of a lot more to break me.

July 15, 1996

W. said I was soft; meant as a compliment. But am I?

My sister Rachel called with the most startling news; 153 Dwight Place (our childhood home where our parents still live), was struck by lightning last night with all our relatives in it. The roof caught on fire, but otherwise, everything is fine.

July 16, 1996

Chilmark. Isabel swims in very cold water. I write haiku while Isabel colors, and not much left to do but play Monopoly and eat dinner.

Bad dreams, of course. Richard is leaving me, Robert, etc.

Wake up wondering about Richard's ambivalence. Where is it? He says he has it, but that I am worth the trade off.

I was rather shocked to discover that he and his old girlfriend T. were on six-month contracts with each other. His idea.

Why do I trust him? Because his behavior towards me has been pristine? Because he wants to marry me? Because I don't care 100% yet?

As soon as I get alone, I get depressed about Robert, can't stop thinking about him.

July 18, 1996

A glorious day up island here at Chilmark. Brilliantly sunny by 8 A.M.

Devon and her family came in from the Cape to visit. Devon took Isabel out deep into the surf, which I am too cowardly to do, and which Isabel loved. Seamus, Devon's husband, was ten when his father died. I really notice that stuff now.

As soon as I get away from Rich, I am inundated by feelings about Robert, which feel more real or more intense or more something.

Call Kath because I feel deranged by it all. Compared to her, I seem like a relationship addict.

I can watch my thoughts for hours these days.

Hope asked Kath, "Do you believe Robert is dead?" He is a person, a ghost, an idea.

A pleasant idleness also afflicts me in this house.

July 22, 1996

As soon as we're alone, Rich and I fuck madly on the floor. Get dressed and go to the wedding in Rockport. Romantic to be with Richard. Dance for a few hours. See a fox in the road coming back.

July 24, 1996

New Jersey

Robert has been dead nine months. If I were pregnant with his death, I'd have given birth to it by now. Pictures of Robert on the wall of his parents' house, and now, rather to my surprise, a blown-up picture of me. I look at the photos of Robert and think of how he was always afraid of the Khmer Rouge in Cambodia, because they attacked people with glasses and took the glasses away.

July 29, 1996

Dreamed Robert had broken up with me. I call him, feeling very upset, at Zen Center. (Why is he always at ZC now that he is dead?) I get him on the phone, hear his voice, suddenly realize he is dead, and oddly, wake up feeling better.

August 8, 1996

Summer seeming to zip along to its close. We're off to Vermont, then leaving in a week.

August 11, 1996

Saw the Perseids last night sitting in lawn chairs with Richard.
He is more sentimental towards me than Robert was.

Two days ago lunch at the Miss Bellows Falls Diner in the
rain. A train. A covered bridge. Yesterday canoes on Silver Lake.
Think of how Robert wanted a canoe. A walk in the woods, a
picnic by the lake.

I need some new shoes. I thought about that this morning
and it made me happy.

Richard saying he feels vulnerable. I don't mind. My turn to
be the host. How I was weaned off Robert in a certain way—not
less committed, but somehow less involved, as if my own health
was a reproach.

Isabel and I returned to Santa Fe in mid-August. We found
the house in good repair. Our kittens had grown into self-pos-
sessed, indoor/outdoor cats. The yard was green after the summer
monsoons.

I decided to move all the rooms around to make it easier for
Rich. I gave Isabel the largest bedroom, which had originally
been Robert's and mine. I cleaned out her former back bedroom
to make a study for Rich. The front bedroom had been Robert's.

I was haunted by my images of him sleeping all day in it, sick
and weak, calling out softly to say *hello*. I decided that the only
way to repossess the room was to move into it. I set it up as a
cheerful bedroom for Rich and me.

Rich began to close up his apartment. He had a yard sale and gave things away. A friend of his helped him drive the Ryder truck cross-country. When he parked it outside my block, the neighbors seemed to appear, as if casually checking out what was happening.

I introduced him as formally as I could to all of them. When I introduced Rich as my fiancé, Norberto—the old guy who had condoled me with *life must go on*—gave me a startling hug. It moved and surprised me. I had always been on super-polite, not hugging, terms with the neighbors, but their honest concern had been apparent.

Rich came through the door, and we fell into bed.

Then we began unpacking and moving into what would be, for all of us, a new life.

Ceremonies

"You're not here—
That much is obvious
By the pot of white orchids
Piñon and spruce
Rustling in the spring wind."

"APOCRYPHA" FROM *The Widow's Coat*

Robert had been dead for a year. The cycle of time came back towards autumn, October. New Mexico put on its fall colors of purple asters and yellow chamisa, brilliant earth foliage beneath a turquoise sky. It was time for another memorial service at the small temple on Cerro Gordo Park.

Robert's mother and sisters came in from the East Coast. They were still devastated, the look on their faces almost as raw as it had been a year before.

I, on the other hand, felt like a different person. I still experienced acute bouts of grief, but they were mixed with an interest in living, with joy at the company of Rich, Isabel, my friends, and the two, large, black cats that now came and went as they pleased. I wouldn't wear black to the memorial service, I decided, but settled on a dark blue, velvet skirt that was patched with designs in rich brocade. It felt right.

Isabel opted to stay home with Rich, much as she had avoided the service after her father's death by going out into the park with my father. She and Rich were negotiating with each other, turning into a parent-and-child pair. When he put his sugar bowl on the kitchen table and took ours off, she was upset.

"Isabel," Rich said, "I've moved a long way to a strange place where I don't feel at home yet. I need some of my own things out. Besides, my mother made this on a potter's wheel for me. Is this OK?"

She nodded, admiring the glaze. They were coming to a lasting accommodation with each other.

The Zen ceremony was a simple one. Jitsudo-sensei kindly came up from Albuquerque to lead it. Tom, Robert's close friend, assisted him in beating on the traditional, wooden, fish-shaped drum and in holding up offerings of sticky rice to the spirit of the deceased.

The ceremony had a cold clean feeling like the splash of salt wave coming in off the north Atlantic. Robert felt truly gone. It didn't matter where or why. There was nothing I or anyone could do about it. But the fact of his death awoke us to life.

Despite the seriousness of his pursuit of the Dharma path, Robert had always been an incorrigible wise guy. When we lived on Rose Alley, around the corner from San Francisco Zen Center, he and I had both been reading *The Blue Cliff Record*, a compendium of koans and commentary. Robert was fascinated by spontaneous gestures meant to unbalance the fixed mind and show reality in a naked form.

One day as I walked around the corner, I saw him standing outside the greengrocer's owned by Zen Center where he worked. Clad in his sturdy green apron, he was enthusiastically watering down crates of fresh produce with a hose. It was a misty, cold San Francisco day, and I was wearing my favorite purple skirt and a jacket.

Robert turned towards me, sprayed the hose on me full blast, and yelled, "Drop off body and mind!"—an exhortation a master might use on a stuck student. But Robert was no master and I was his wife, now wet and extremely irritated.

As I sat cross-legged listening to the sutras being chanted at Robert's memorial service, I realized that his death had had the desired effect of that cold hose on me. I would never be the same person. I wondered a bit nostalgically if I would ever return to a certain ease of mind, not quite realizing that I was still in a process of grief, and that in years to come my emotions would indeed be less troubled.

But I felt different in a positive way. Although I resisted believing that any good could come of Robert's death, it had given me a new appreciation of life.

After the ceremony, we broke for tea and cookies in the living room. I saw many old friends, Buddhist practitioners, and just people in our wide community who had wanted to be there.

I also saw Bill for the first time in months.

"So, where's first boy?" he asked, using the nickname he had given Rich, sight unseen.

"At home with Isabel. Paying his debt to a dead man." No woman could talk to Bill for long without flirting.

"Miriam," he said in a slow distinct voice. "I tried to pay a debt to a dead man. *With you.*"

I started laughing. "Next lifetime, Billy," I said.

When I repeated this to a friend, she was horrified. "Now you'll be reincarnated with him!" she exclaimed.

There were worse fates, I thought. It just wasn't my fate for this lifetime.

Richard, Isabel, and I settled into an easy groove. He found work in Albuquerque with the same employer he had had in Boston, and despite the commute, seemed glad to have found steady employment without an elaborate search. We cooked, played games, listened to the radio, visited my friends, and put up houseguests, who had come to visit from Boston. We began to travel all over New Mexico and into southern Colorado, enjoying hot springs, deserts, caverns, ruins, mountains, and tiny cafes nestled against the immensity of the road. We felt like a family.

I had settled most of the aspects of Robert's estate, except that I resisted finally closing his savings account. It lost money to a fee every month, which was a ridiculous waste, but still I felt as if I were trespassing.

Robert and I had never been able to agree about money. He earned little and enjoyed spending. I was the responsible one, the ant to his grasshopper, and I had supported us for years. In one of those weird psychological twists all too familiar to marriage, the dynamic was that he resented me, found me controlling and stingy. I really didn't think that was the case, but Robert was dead, and any real dialogue between us on this or any other topic was now impossible.

In an odd way that was one of the most upsetting things about being widowed: I was unable to resolve fights and issues that had gone on for years, quarreling with a ghost. Instead, for a year and a half I couldn't bring myself to touch Robert's dwindling account of less than a thousand dollars, his entire fiscal estate.

The history of the money itself was also somewhat upsetting. Robert had been given a much larger amount by an elderly friend, an ailing Zen priest, for safekeeping. But Robert, irresponsible as always, had gradually "borrowed" from the account, but never repaid any of it. I was terrified by the inevitable day of reckoning, but Robert kept taking the money. When he fell ill and stayed that way, the friend told him to keep the money as a gift. Once again, Robert had managed without dire consequences.

Friends and family weren't Robert's only tangled financial relationships. He often gave the wrong social security number due to a state of ill-defined paranoia.

"I only change one digit," he would say. "That way I can claim it was a computer error."

He was also never motivated to pay his debts, whether to the gas company, the federal government, or me. Paying joint taxes with him was a nightmare; sharing a credit card, an impossibility. Handling money together was the main thing about our life together that I did not miss.

Armed with a death certificate, I showed up at the main branch of the bank on the Plaza. The Plaza was not crowded at that season, with just some bundled-up locals crossing it in the chilly breeze. A light winter wind swirled dead leaves in a tiny dust devil.

The bank was happy to help me close out the account. Checking the social security number, they found it was off by one digit. Hearing Robert's voice in my mind, I just shrugged and looked baffled. Even in death, Robert could madden me. As it was obviously the correct account, and I, the widow, they closed it and gave me the money. I had fully intended to deposit it in Isabel's college savings account.

But the windy day, the social security number, and the odd feeling that I had finally gotten some money from Robert were overwhelming. I crossed the Plaza and walked into Packard's, the famous dealer in Indian art and jewelry. I had often admired the gleaming black-ware pots from Santa Clara Pueblo there, and the delicate needlepoint turquoise work from the Zuni.

Without hesitating, I decided to buy myself a very expensive pair of turquoise earrings. I settled on a contemporary pair in the shape of flowers, with each petal a different color of turquoise stone. Then I spent the rest on a heavy cuff bracelet of Navajo work in silver, which I knew Kath would wear. She was back in town after her year in Korea and staying with friends.

Then I called her on the phone and said, "Come over; I have something for you. Robert bought us some very fancy and expensive jewelry and I want you to see."

Clothes in general, new clothes in particular, had become something of an obsession of mine since Robert's death. I had become seized with the obsession that I should gradually replace all my old clothes with new ones until I was clad entirely in items that postdated Robert. Of course, this was not exactly practical, and I hung on to my coats and boots, vintage dresses, scarves, and earrings. But I did buy as many new clothes as I could afford, and I threw out the outfits I had worn to Robert's memorial, to the cremation, and even what I had worn to the ICU when he was in a coma. I also bought lots of new slinky nightgowns, cute pajamas, and a pile of underwear. Somehow I felt these items should not overlap between Robert and Richard.

It reminded me of the small shopping spree I went on soon after giving birth to Isabel. I had been on a much tighter budget in those days, and all I'd been able to afford was a short black skirt and a dozen underpants, but I'd felt different, much as I did now, and wanted to mark the occasion with new clothes.

It seemed perhaps a trivial and materialistic pursuit, but I had been raised in a coat manufacturing family. Because my father owned the company, we got new coats and jackets—usually off the sample racks—with every seasonal change but summer.

As an adult, I was the only person I knew who longed for a new spring coat, something which had long gone out of fashion. For me, new clothes were an atavistic symbol of new life.

That spring I received the disturbing news that Baker-roshi wanted to inter some of Robert's ashes at the monastery in Crestone, Colorado. I hadn't seen Richard Baker-roshi since Robert's forty-nine day ceremony, and I had very negative feelings about the monastery, which sat in admittedly scenic surroundings at the base of a range of the southern Rockies. Robert had spent many months practicing in the Crestone monastery, often to the great disruption of our family life.

When Isabel was three, he went for a hundred days of monastic practice. Isabel and I commuted every other week to see him, often in the harsh winter weather that lurked around the enormous lumpy mountain of San Antonio or through the San Luis valley, which often had the lowest recorded temperature in the nation.

It was a time of great stress for us. We lived together in one room, which alternately was freezing cold, boiling hot, or stank of propane. Meals were a confused affair, with the monks eating formally, Isabel and I scrounging in the kitchen. In fact, as many people, from moms to monks, were happy to point out: children and monasteries just didn't go together. It was a failed experiment, and, in part, led to Robert leaving his teacher, Baker-roshi.

Paradoxically, it was Baker-roshi, with his optimism about Buddhism in America and his genuine enthusiasm for children, who was the only one who had encouraged us. Isabel would have fond memories of riding on his shoulders or visiting his room, cluttered with statues and Buddhist paraphernalia.

I did not have fond memories of the monastery, however. I had quarreled with the community about everything from money to an overflowing septic system. I had felt discounted as a woman, a mother, and a non-Zen student. The truth was I had no right or reason to be there. I had simply been following

Robert and attempting to keep the family together. I had zero wish to return there.

Still, I did not feel I could forbid them their burial of Robert's ashes, even if Robert had left under a cloud of ambivalence and never returned. After all, bits of Robert's ashes were now being carried around in the pouches of old hippies and scattered in poet's gardens. After Miriam B. had divided them, I had let go of their fate. I still had my share in the ugly container hidden in a corner of my study.

By extension of my relationship, I felt I needed to be present at the ceremony in Crestone.

Robert himself had loved Buddhist ceremonies of all kinds. He felt they created an actual space in which things could change and happen.

I was haunted by a strange memory of a ceremony involving Issan Dorsey. Issan had been a wild man, a drag queen, a drug addict. Then he became a Zen priest. He was a kindly, hilarious person, who also had a sharp witty edge. But never quite having abandoned his self-destructive ways, he had a love affair with a young crazy who often lived on the street, which probably led to their having AIDS at a time when the prevention of the disease was common knowledge. They both died, and we mourned Issan.

Before he died, when he was quite ill, he came to Santa Fe from San Francisco to complete some training with Baker-roshi.

Robert still had his long beard in those days, before he was a clean-shaven monk.

It was an August night. In the early evening, I washed dishes. My back to the door, I faced the window, over the kitchen sink, through which I could see the full moon rise through the leafy branches of the neighbor's Chinese elm—whose roots periodically ruined our plumbing.

Robert came in and put his arms around me from behind.

He was helping Baker-roshi with a ceremony, a Dharma transmission for Issan. The ceremony would confirm that Issan had the mind of a Buddha, which was already apparent to those around him. There was no longer even a thin membrane of tissue between that of Issan's brain and that of Shakyamuni Buddha sitting beneath a tree somewhere very dry on the subcontinent of India.

The problem was Robert needed a small tin box. The problem was Issan had AIDS, and this ceremony—I gathered because I wasn't allowed to know—involved cutting Issan with a razor to release some drops of his blood. His blood was full of a lethal virus out of equatorial Africa via the Castro and upper Polk Street. Somehow the contaminated razor would have to be disposed of.

Robert looked everywhere, no small box. Then he happened upon my coffee tin—the brightly colored one holding Italian mint mocha from General Foods International Coffees.

"I need the tin," he said, shaking out the rich mix into an old yogurt container, rinsing, and pocketing the International Coffee box.

I've always wondered—What became of the razor, bloody, and the green-and-blue tin? Did Robert bury them? Or put them in the trash? Looking back, I don't even trust my own memory. Maybe that razor was simply used to shave Issan's head rather than something more lurid. That was just one more question I had no way to ask and have answered, any more than I could ask Robert why he always lied about his social security number or where he and Issan had gone.

And now I had to set off for Crestone with Miriam B. and a great feeling of trepidation.

Rich, never one to let an opportunity for fun or travel pass, set up an itinerary. I would go to Crestone, and he and Isabel would meet me in Alamosa, Colorado, a midway point. We'd sleep there, then have a nice time the next day at the Great Sand Dunes. I would spend only a few hours at the monastery.

In keeping with my new clothes policy, I had an outfit picked out—black pants and a new camp shirt in black and white rayon, printed with mystical moons and suns. There was something talismanic about the shirt, and I wore it for protection.

As soon as I was back on that familiar patch of land, beautiful arid country of juniper and piñon, flanked by snow-covered cliffs and grand mountains, my stomach clenched. Immediately, things began to go wrong for me. I had made it clear that I could only stay for only a few hours, but the ceremony, in traditional Baker-roshi fashion, was running hours late. I seemed to have no option but to hang around.

Robert's sisters and mother had come again from a great distance and again were in the acute throes of grief. It depressed me to be so out-of-synch with his family. I loved them, and we had shared a loss. His sisters were special women, beautiful, creative, warm. But my recovery seemed like nothing but a reproach to them.

I had recently told my friend Ana that I had stopped missing Robert as a *role*, father or husband. I told her I just missed him, his conversation, and his observations.

Ana said something very profound to me, "You miss the only thing you ever really possessed."

Although rationally Robert's sisters could see that a normalizing life was good for Isabel, I still felt judged.

"God," I said, "I'm just so irritated being here. This place really gets on my nerves."

"Do you want a Valium? Xanax?" a family member inquired anxiously, as if my irritation might turn homicidal. I had to laugh to myself. At least, mercifully, I wasn't medicating every negative emotion.

Finally I decided I would leave at a certain time, ceremony or no ceremony. I had promised Rich and Isabel I would be at the Best Western at an appointed time. Once again the monastery threatened to come between me and my child's needs.

Then the ceremony began, with Baker-roshi and a few attendants winding dramatically through the scrub of the mountainside to the ringing of a small bell gong. A beautifully shaped stone, formed like a small mountain, was prepared over a small open pit. Robert's ashes were set beside it, and in an oddly visceral ceremony, we took turns pouring Robert's ashes through a funnel of red and silver paper into the ground.

Just as we were starting, a large black dog appeared out of nowhere and started drinking water out of a ritual bowl. It was the moment of the ceremony Robert would have liked best.

Otherwise, I was filled with uncharitable thoughts: Robert's interment was just to show the junior monks the proper way to bury someone. Robert wouldn't have wanted to be here.

Displays of acute grief from Robert's family made me feel guilty and inadequate. A year and a half after his death, my grief had mellowed. And Baker-roshi didn't seem to know any more about death than your average person.

I was desperate to get out of there. Besides, I was now about to be several hours late. I called the motel and left a message for Rich and Isabel and hopped in the car. As soon as we reached the perimeter of the property, my body relaxed. Actually, I stank; a cold sweat had been leaking from my pores ever since I arrived.

By the time we reached the motel in Alamosa, I was exhausted. Richard and Isabel were very worried, having never gotten my message. Isabel in particular was distraught and weepy. Once again, I cursed the monastery for interfering with my mothering.

But this time I was clearer; it was my fault. No one had forced me to stay, and I was not a Zen student nor married to one. Everything I had passively put up with over the years now seemed a lot more like my own responsibility. I knew I would never go back to the monastery.

The next day, on the trip to the Great Sand Dunes, I felt that I was reclaiming a relationship to the beauty of the austere San Luis Valley, which lay between two enormous, snow-covered ranges. The sand dunes rose like a majestic mirage, and we ran up and rolled down them along with other cheerful sightseers. A tiny stream ran along the perimeter, with a mysterious, tidal bore that created waves every few minutes. It was freezing cold on our newly bare feet.

About that time, Rich and I decided to get married. By our wedding, we would have all been living together in Santa Fe for a year, and Robert would have been dead for two. We were in a private and delighted space about our decision.

Then came the necessity of wedding plans. Robert and I had eloped when we were married, and our families had not been invited. As a result, my mother and sisters were still quite mad at me about the topic, as were numerous of my friends. Rich himself wanted to invite all his friends and family; he wanted a big party, in part because he had never been married before. And I felt that the community that had supported me when Robert died needed to eat and drink and dance together one more time to mark the transition. So it seemed as if we would need a big wedding. The only problem was, I hated the idea.

The first time I was married, I eloped in part because I didn't want to be a Bride with a capital B. I told myself that it was because I was not a piece of property in a patriarchal institution (I actually still talked like that then), and therefore, I was not going to change my name or wear a ring. But it was also because I was afraid of being criticized or judged. I was afraid someone would tell me I looked fat, that my bad hair was worse, that my hippie dress was hideous. So with a minimum of wedding, I plunged straight into marriage.

Now fifteen years later, I was planning a wedding, complete with rabbi, that cost more than it would to renovate my crumbling bathroom or install a really good drip irrigation system. If not a traditional bride, I was certainly going to be some kind of bride. I even bought a white hat with a tiny veil.

Richard, a person who liked categories, had asked, would I . . .

A. marry him

B. have a ritual ceremony

C. give a party

I happily said yes to A, agreed to B, and with some fear, said yes on C, as well.

What I mostly said yes to was catering. At first, I resisted. I had an image of a brief affair, in which my guests snacked lightly and then went out to dinner on their own. An old friend accused me of planning to serve just trays of Triscuits and olives. As a result of my resistance to catering, I found myself sobbing over a nice deli counter, because Rich had gently suggested that maybe we needed to feed our families—who would have come thousands of miles—an actual meal.

"Why are you crying?" he asked.

"I'm crying because Robert is dead, and if he were still alive, I wouldn't be having this stupid conversation about feeding all those people."

Luckily, Rich was able to take this in stride and patted me gently until I calmed down.

One of the main reasons I was willing to go with a real wedding was that I knew Isabel, now eight years old, would like it. And it would help us feel like a family of three. Her name was on the invitation, and a pink organdy dress hung ready for her self-described role as "best woman." In her mind, the wedding served as a transition in her relationship with Richard from what she called "a fatherish friend" to an official stepfather. So in a way, we were all getting married together.

And so the wedding was planned.

My old friend Carol offered us the use of her field, an exquisite piece of property with a view to the west of the Jemez Mountains. She had gotten divorced when I was widowed, and in a pleasant twist of fate, she had also fallen in love and married that summer. The home of newlyweds seemed an auspicious spot for a wedding, and we rented a big tent to put up in the field.

We asked Lynn Gottlieb to perform the ceremony. Rich liked her inclusive approach, her casual old-hippie manner, her use of some Native American imagery mixed in with Judaism. I liked her and the fact that she had been with me when Robert died.

In our marriage vows, Rich and I could not agree exactly on the wording. Rich included, "I take you with all your faults and strengths as I offer myself to you with all my faults and strengths."

There was no way I was going to say that. Although his vow was a model of acceptance, I wasn't going to admit I had faults, particularly not in front of all those guests. So I left that part out of my vow.

I was having an interesting experience in preparing for this marriage; it was forcing me to observe myself in a different way. I was more able simply to watch my reactions towards Rich than I ever had been with Robert, and hence, we had a more peaceful relationship.

The endless nagging of the wives around me towards their husbands—once very familiar, despite its old-fashioned tone—now seemed futile. After all, I told myself, I nagged Robert for thirteen years, and it did no good. I nagged him about stupid things, important things, things I just thought were important. I nagged and nagged, and he never changed. I nagged until he went into a coma and died, and I realized, once and for all, its utter futility.

I was trying to be different with Rich. But I was tested. Rich—unconscious of the effect it would have—put a large can of foot powder with bold lettering extolling its anti-itch properties on his night table next to the bed. I might envision a scented candle here—or a vase of flowers—but foot powder was not on my list. My undying love was instantly replaced with extreme irritation. In my first marriage I would have blurted out the truth: Get that offensive foot powder out of my sight—and I mean now! But life and loss had taught me a modicum of tolerance. I said nothing.

A friend of mine, upon hearing this story, said, "Every relationship has its foot powder moments!" My therapist, who had been Robert's and my couple's counselor, claimed that people become more homicidal over housework—the correct way to tie a garbage bag, for example—than over much more serious issues.

It took Carol to point out what my own foot powder issue was. I mentioned that both my husbands had complained that I didn't wrap cheese properly before I put it back in the refrigerator. How odd, I mused, that I'd managed to take up with two men who shared this strange attention to detail. As she had once lived in my house for several weeks and knew me well,

Carol said, "You don't wrap the cheese properly. It dries out. You don't pay attention."

I could hardly believe it, but I started laughing. Perhaps I was not the only one who practiced tolerance.

A few weeks before the wedding, Rich and I set out to buy each other gifts. I still didn't like wearing a ring, but Jewish tradition suggested that marriage was created, in part, by a gift of value. So we went to Sissell's, the fabulous, discount jewelry store on the strip where Indian jewelry of all descriptions—from turquoise-and-silver, squash-blossom necklaces to inlaid earrings—hung from floor to ceiling. We browsed, looking for a bolo tie for Rich and for a Zuni fetish necklace for me. I had long coveted one of these many-stranded necklaces hung with numerous, tiny, carved animals—birds, bears—in semi-precious stone.

Isabel found the perfect one with a large, turquoise bear pendant hanging from the bottom.

At the cash register, a pleasant, Native American woman commented on what we were buying and asked about the occasion.

When I told her a bit of the story, she put her face in her hands and almost sobbing, exclaimed, "I just don't know what to do!"

"About what?" I asked.

" I was married pretty young . . . I've got a teen-age daughter. My husband and I split up about three years ago. Now there's this guy I went out with in high school."

"Is he nice?"

"Nice! He's a wonderful person! Kind, considerate, has a good job."

"What's the problem?"

"Well, he wants to marry me. I'm not sure; maybe it's too soon. He gets on great with my daughter; I've known him forever. What do you think I should do?"

"Marry him," I said, and we all started laughing, as I bought Richard's gift, and he, mine.

The wedding plans continued, and on Labor Day weekend our families and out-of-town friends descended. Devon, who had been very mad to be excluded from my first marriage's elopement, came from Delaware, her second trip west to see me in less than two years.

The families planned the rehearsal dinner in a nice Italian restaurant. This was a scene of some concern to me, as rehearsal dinners in my family were usually boisterous in the extreme, with toasts bordering on the dubious boundaries of taste. This proved to be the case now, as well.

One of my sisters confessed that "everything I learned about love and sex came from reading Richard and Miriam's letters when they were teenagers."

Various people had to be restrained from going on at length about my dead husband and what a relief it was that Rich had appeared to marry me.

My brother cited Rich as his inspiration for sleeping naked.

It went on from there, but luckily, in my mind at least, little of it was preserved for posterity on the video that highlighted mostly the food and shots of chatting relatives.

The day of the wedding, in the bustle of my house, I realized that it was, indeed, the flip of a funeral. The cast of characters was similar, and the emotional intensity, though not as great, was still there. Kath might have well remarked, "This is like a funeral, only much, much happier."

Devon had arranged my flowers into an exquisite, country-wedding bouquet. She tied Richard's bowtie ceremoniously. Juliet stopped by for five minutes, squinted at my face, applied eyeliner, eye shadow, and blush, and departed like a hummingbird. The caterers had suggested we select an emergency team for the wedding, so if some child broke an arm or a guest fell down drunk, the bride and groom would not have to be the ones to rush to the hospital. Devon, her husband Seamus, and Kath were happy to be chosen.

We arrived at Carol's field in good time. Balloons marked the country mailbox and entrance. Rabbi Lynn banged on her tambourine to start the ceremony. Isabel walked down the grassy aisle looking angelic in the cloud of the organdy dress my mother had specially ordered for her from an old-fashioned Italian bride shop in New Jersey. Before the ceremony, Isabel had fussed at the dress, even though she had chosen it with my mother: it itched, it was horrible, embarrassing.

"Let her fuss about the dress," Devon whispered in my ear, "rather than something more important." We knew that the day, though joyful, would also be hard for her.

Still, she rallied as flower girl, walking firmly and throwing her posies with the force of a pro-ball pitcher.

She, Richard, and I stood under the huppah, the traditional Jewish shelter for bride and groom. The huppah is by its nature temporary and tent-like. Ours was composed of four poles, holding up my maternal grandfather's prayer shawl, which he had brought from Russia. He, of course, had been an atheist and a socialist, but his tallis still retained the magic of the past.

Holding on to the poles as the shawl billowed in the breeze were four friends: Kath was there for me, Sharon, who had brought Rabbi Lynn to Robert's deathbed, Richard's old girlfriend T., who had been his most serious relationship besides me, and a close friend of his from Boston, a tall shy man, who seemed happier to hold a pole than to speak during the ceremony.

The ceremony commenced with our reading our vows, circling each other seven times in traditional fashion, and exchanging our gifts. We gave Isabel an enormous, expensive doll she had been coveting and finally, relieved of her ritual duties, she ran off to sit with her friends. Family and friends showered us with seven blessings. As the ceremony ended, the band struck up, and everyone threw hard candy.

We followed an ancient custom of Judaism, for the bride and groom to sequester themselves for a few minutes between the ceremony and the party. We sat in Carol's living room, drinking champagne and eating strawberries, high on bliss. Then Isabel came bursting in to the seclusion, stripped off the loathsome itchy dress, changed into a pair of shorts, and ran back outside to show off her doll.

After that, the wedding party was perhaps like any other, notable for its small moments of humor and happiness. There were numerous tiny tableaux: two of Richard's old girlfriends talking to each other, Hope wearing a big daisy in her hair and dancing with her little girl Pearl, Rich eating cake, two wedding guests, who would soon decide to have a baby, dancing off by themselves to music only they could hear, waltzing as the rest of us line danced to klezmer.

We left portable cameras on the table, and although we developed many festive snapshots, some of them were very odd. Some child had documented the portable toilet, in detail. Someone had taken numerous photos of a barbed-wire fence. There was a pleasant-looking woman, eating cake, whom no one has ever been able to identify. And there was a black shadow figure, looking like Death in Bergman's *The Seventh Seal,* looming over a field before the guests arrived. There was also a snapshot of the little altar with photographs of us as teenagers, which Rich suddenly decided looked like a memorial to two adolescent lovers who had died young.

The party continued until dark. I knew it was a success when I saw Devon, Seamus, and Kath boogying together and exclaiming, "We didn't have to go to the emergency room!"

As dusk fell, we packed up the leftover champagne and drove up the mountain to Ten Thousand Waves, the Japanese-style hot tubs, where we had rented two large pools to accommodate our guests. About thirty-five people soaked in the hot water beneath the stars.

I lay back in the water, my head still full of the image of my guests dancing around the tent and I running in a line in my stocking feet because my shoes got too tight. I had ruined my silky socks with rips and grass stains. But I could still see us dancing.

The Mustard Seed

"I never found that mustard seed
Nor did the woman in the story
Who heard tale after tale of loss and sorrow
Knocking on the turquoise doors of a thousand dusty
*   villages."*

"AFTER YOU" FROM *Archeology of Desire*

Epilogue

There is a Buddhist teaching story about a woman whose only
child dies. I think there is also a Japanese version of the tale, in
which an old, childless couple, who dote on their cat, also lose it
to death. In any case, a desperately bereaved woman comes to
Shakyamuni Buddha, asking for a miracle, asking, "Please bring
my child back to life." The Buddha agrees, but only if she will
bring him a mustard seed from a household that has never known
death. And so the woman goes out seeking.

A mustard seed is a tiny thing, but a pungent one. In the New Testament, Jesus also referred to a mustard seed, saying that faith in that minuscule amount could move mountains. This seed is small, but powerful.

I imagine the bereaved mother knocking on the doors of a thousand houses in a hundred villages and asking first, "Have you known death?"

Of course, the answer is yes, and she hears the stories of old people passing quietly, babies like hers dead, children struck down by illness, women in childbirth, men in their prime felled by a flash of lightning or an accident, cattle gone, even fruit trees dying in droughts or of blight or age.

How long does she keep knocking before it dawns on her why she has been sent: to discover she is not alone.

In my private imagination, there is more than one version. In the first, she keeps hoping that somewhere she will find the blessed household where she can ask her second question: Do you have a mustard seed? In the other, her grief is healed when she accepts the common lot of the community of all living things.

After my husband Robert died, I did both things. I looked with envy and jealousy at those I believed had never suffered, and yet I found everywhere that no one had a household from which I could beg even a tiny seed.

Right after Robert died, my friend Margo came through the door to pay a condolence call, holding up a small offering of our mutually favorite cookies, Milano mint. I looked at Margo. She looked the same as always—curly black hair, an indefinable chic I always attributed to having lived in France—and suddenly I saw her as if for the first time. I had known her for many years, but before that, when she was very young, her husband, a Frenchman, had been killed in an accident, leaving her a widow with a tiny baby. I had, of course, known all this, but it had just been a vague romance, part of her mystique. Suddenly, I realized what she had gone through. We both started crying as we embraced, tears of recognition, as if we were long-lost relatives who had met for the first time.

I continued to try to accept Robert's death and to move on.

A psychic who was a friend of mine tried to contact my dead husband Robert in the great beyond. "He says he hasn't reincarnated," she reported, "because he doesn't believe in it."

This was true. I used to throw myself on him as a romantic gesture in the days before he was sick and try to make him promise we'd be born together one more time. He'd always refuse, shoving me off gently. Although Robert was a Buddhist monk in a tradition that definitely believed in reincarnation, he always subscribed to the words of the Buddha, who had apparently told his followers not to worry about such things, but to "work diligently on your own salvation" now.

When I felt blue, I turned to my cat Orpheo more than to any person, even than to Richard. I loved Orpheo more than any cat I had ever had. He had long, black, feathery fur and brilliant green eyes. He grew enormously plump, affectionate, lazy. If I cried or just felt sad, he would come and lie on me, barely purring but staring adoringly. I secretly became convinced that he was my dead husband, reincarnated as a cat, come back to keep a compassionate eye on me.

Then, after I remarried and was living happily with Richard, Orpheo disappeared one early autumn day. I was sure he was gone forever—a consoling cat who had vanished now that I no longer lived beneath the sign of grief.

Sixteen days later, as I awoke from a nap, I saw Orpheo coming in the cat door. I thought I was hallucinating. He was filthy but still fat. Beneath his claws were pads of foam rubber. Perhaps he'd been locked in a kids' tree house or taken in by the vagrants, who lived in cardboard shacks down by the tracks. Wherever he had been, he was happy to be back. For several days, he followed me about like a dog, then settled into his old routines.

As my daughter and I petted him on the bed one evening, she shocked me by saying, "I think Dad got reborn as Orpheo." It was as if she had read my mind. Still, I had lately become skeptical, thinking that Robert would probably not have wanted to come back as anything without testicles.

Instead, I suggested, "Orpheo doesn't lead a very exciting life. Do you think Dad would want to be so mellow?"

"Dad's last life was exciting," she said. "Maybe he wants a quieter life." Then inspiration struck. "I know who Dad came back as!" she shouted.

"Who?" I wanted to know.

"Richard!" she yelled, "Dad came back as Richard!"

Rich laughed from the next room where he was reading the newspaper. He'd been born in 1953; Robert, in 1959. But many things had indeed come back into our lives.

The black cat turned over to have his stomach scratched.

In my creative writing classes, before Robert had died, I often gave an assignment to write to a dead person. "Say hello," I'd urge. "Tell them what's new, how you feel." Then I'd be gratified if the students were moved to tears as they poured out their feelings.

I stopped being able to give the assignment after I was bereaved, but I wrote to Robert, anyway.

Dear Robert,

I often remember the Safeway at Church and Market. That was the first place I ever saw a punk with that prison tattoo—L-O-V-E written one letter per finger of the left hand and H-A-T-E on the fingers of the right. The thumbs were naked, as if leaving their options open.

Since you died, that is how I am, H-A-T-E and L-O-V-E. I think of all the bad things you did to me, like spending up to my Master Card limit and never paying me back. Things that you never apologized for and never intended to apologize for. Then I move to L-O-V-E, how you gave me a daughter with your rows of double eyelashes and how you loved me for myself.

I haven't been to San Francisco since you died, but we are going in March. I'm sure the Safeway is gone, no longer full of men in leather and nipple clips in broad daylight.

Really, we're all fine, better than to be expected. See you.
Love,
Miriam

I wrote to him even years after he died.

Dear Robert,

Last night I had a dream about you I didn't appreciate. It was the usual; you'd been in a coma for four years. I was married to Rich, you woke up, dropped me for another girlfriend, and we weren't on good terms. In this dream you were still trying to get me into bed, and although I agreed to make love, I said, "You'll never possess me again."

"How do you know?" you said.

"Because I've spent forty-five years trapped in this body, and if there is one thing I know, it is the inside of my own head."

Then we started quarreling because Rich and I had decided to move to northern California, and you were very upset because you and I had joint-custody of our daughter Isabel, but you saw her only on Thursdays at your sister's house, because you had to work so hard and were broke. And I got frightened you'd kidnap her, and I'd never see her again.

I'm sorry, Berto, that dead you work so hard, which you never did in life, and that you are so busy with girlfriends and sisters that you can hardly visit our daughter. I wish our joint-custody—you dead, me living—would go more smoothly, although in my waking hours I believe that somehow you do look out for our child.

I don't know why your ghost doesn't rest as I myself wander through the realms of sleep. Truly, I wish I could be kinder in my dreams to both of us.

Love,
Miriam

About three years after Robert's death, I had my most profound experience of looking for a mustard seed. I was dimly aware that two sisters from the prep school in town had died in a car crash in California, en route to college. Several of my creative writing students at the Community College had been their friends, written poems for them, gone to the funeral, wept in class. But I didn't realize who they were until I walked into my favorite Chinese restaurant and saw their photograph on the cash register, with a note about a scholarship fund. They were the daughters of the proprietor and his wife.

Robert and I had often frequented that restaurant. It was in a strip mall, but the food was good, and everyone always smiled at baby Isabel, even when she ended up throwing a pile of fried rice on the floor or secreting an egg roll in the back of a booth. Once, one waitress, who was an ethnic Buddhist from somewhere in East Asia, had refused to take money from Robert for his meal, because she had recognized him as a Buddhist priest.

Now I was devastated to realize that these kindly people had been bereaved by the death of both their children.

The owners were visibly absent for several months, but one day when I went in to pick up a take-out order, I saw the proprietor standing behind the cash register and knew I had to say something. I went up to him and waited for him to finish with another customer. He could see by my face what I wanted to say.

"I'm so sorry, about your daughters. . . . I'm so sorry." I, the expert on grief, was tongue-tied. "I don't know if you knew . . . my husband died a few years ago. . . . I'm sorry."

"I know they are all OK," he said.

"How do you go on, you and your wife? Show up in the morning?"

"We were trained for hard work," he said. "That's how we were raised."

We were both sobbing, and then we were holding hands across the counter, rocking back and forth.

"I know they are all OK," he repeated.

It was so similar to what Baker-roshi had said at the forty-nine-day ceremony, when he'd said, "Robert, we are all taking care of ourselves and hope you are too."

But soon I took my savory-smelling bag of Chinese food, paid, and left the restaurant's dim interior.

Back out in the bright light and heat of the parking lot, I could see the mountains behind me. Soon the first snow would appear on them, just as it did every autumn. But now, it was still hot and dusty in town, the fields golden with wild sunflowers.

Bibliography

Poetry

Archeology Of Desire, Red Hen, 2001

Inadvertent Altar, La Alameda Press, 2000

The Widow's Coat, Ahsahta Press, 1999, 2002

The Art Of Love: New And Selected Poems, La Alameda Press, 1994

Pocahontas Discovers America, Adastra Press, 1993

True Body, Parallax Press, 1991

Acequia Madre: Through The Mother Ditch, Adastra Press, 1988

Aegean Doorway, Zephyr Press, 1984

Books On Writing

Unbroken Line: Writing In the Lineage Of Poetry (Sherman Asher Publishing, 1999)

Fiction And Memoir

Dirty Laundry: 100 Days In A Zen Monastery With Robert Winson (La Alameda Press, 1997; New World Library 1999)

Coastal Lives: A Novel (Center Press, 1991)

Editor

Another Desert: Jewish Poetry Of New Mexico (Sherman Asher Publishing 1998, With Joan Logghe)

Canoeing Down Cabarga Creek: Buddhist Poems Of Philip Whalen (Parallax Press, 1996, With Robert Winson)

New Mexico Poetry Renaissance: 41 Poets, A Community On Paper (Red Crane, 1994, With Sharon Niederman)